BAPTISM
WHAT IS IT GOOD FOR?

BAPTISM
WHAT IS IT GOOD FOR?

By
Edward James Wittlif

BAPTISM
WHAT IS IT GOOD FOR?

Published by
© 2021 by Edward James Wittlif

All Scriptures are taken from the NEW AMERICAN STANDARD (NAS) unless otherwise noted: Scripture taken from the NEW AMERICAN STANDARD BIBLE®, copyright© 1960, 1962, 1963, 1968, 1971, 1972, 1973, 1975, 1977, 1995 by The Lockman Foundation. Used by permission.

Scriptures marked NIV are taken from the NEW INTERNATIONAL VERSION (NIV): Scripture taken from THE HOLY BIBLE, NEW INTERNATIONAL VERSION ®. Copyright© 1973, 1978, 1984 by International Bible Society. Used by permission of Zondervan.

Scriptures marked ESV are taken from the ENGLISH STANDARD VERSION (ESV): Scripture quotations are from The ESV ® Bible (The Holy Bible, English Standard Version®), copyright © 2001 by Crossway, a publishing ministry of Good News Publishers. Used by permission. All rights reserved.

ALL RIGHTS RESERVED
No part of the publication may be reproduced, stored in a retrieval system, or transmitted, in any form or by any means — electronic, mechanical, photocopying, recording, or otherwise — without prior written permission.

Scripture references are written giving Book, Chapter, and Verse/s, A lower-case letter following the verse means that I am quoting only a portion of the verse. The letter used indicates the position within the verse where the quote starts. This is done to provide emphasis where necessary.

ISBN: 978-0-578-93252-1

DEDICATION:

To my Lord and my God, Jesus my Redeemer. I pray that this book will bring Him glory and serve His purpose.

To my mentors in the faith Warren Wilcox and Roy Lanier, Sr., who taught me to study and especially to question rather than simply accept what others say. They showed me that God by His nature wants us to question and study and grow in knowledge which leads us to a sure knowledge of Him and His will. In this way our confidence is based on the firm foundation, Jesus Christ.

To my brothers in the Lord Rob Redden and Joseph Slater for their reviews and suggestions for my manuscript.

To my beloved wife, Donna for her encouragement and support throughout this project.

Table Of Content

INTRODUCTION 1

CHAPTER ONE:
WHAT IS NECESSARY FOR SALVATION? 7

CHAPTER TWO:
SAVED BY GRACE 12

CHAPTER THREE:
THE OLD COVENANT VERSUS THE NEW
COVENANT 35

CHAPTER FOUR:
JOHN THE BAPTIST'S BAPTISM WAS DURING THE
OLD COVENANT 41

CHAPTER FIVE:
JESUS IS BAPTIZED BY JOHN 46

CHAPTER SIX:
SAVED BY FAITH: IS IT ENOUGH? 53

CHAPTER SEVEN:
HEARING THE GOSPEL: THE BASIS FOR FAITH 70

CHAPTER EIGHT:
SAVED BY REPENTANCE 77

CHAPTER NINE:
SAVED BY CONFESSING JESUS AS LORD 86

CHAPTER TEN:
SAVED BY BAPTISM 91

CHAPTER ELEVEN:
AN EXAMINATION OF MATTHEW 28:18-20 97

CHAPTER TWELVE:
JESUS AND GOD'S WORK IN OUR BAPTISM 101

CHAPTER THIRTEEN:
WHY DO WE NEED JESUS? 119

CHAPTER FOURTEEN:
HOW IS BAPTISM ADMINISTERED? 136

CHAPTER FIFTEEN:
WHAT THE CHRISTIAN WRITERS OF THE FIRST,
SECOND, AND THIRD CENTURIES SAY ABOUT
BAPTISM 145

CHAPTER SIXTEEN:
BORN AGAIN 154

CHAPTER SEVENTEEN:
ROMANS SIX: A DEEPER LOOK 160

CHAPTER EIGHTEEN:
WASHING OUR ROBES 181

CHAPTER NINETEEN:
COMMITMENT 190

CHAPTER TWENTY:
IN CONCLUSION 198

SPECIAL STUDIES 207

A1 THE NEW TESTAMENT HAS FIVE DIFFERENT
BAPTISMS 208

A2 CONVERSIONS AND GROWTH OF THE CHURCH IN ACTS 221

A3 CORNELIUS RECEIVING THE SPIRIT PRIOR TO BAPTISM...234

A4 INFANT BAPTISM AND ORIGINAL SIN 240

A5 ME IN CHRIST VERSUS CHRIST IN ME 247

A6 BAPTISM FOR THE DEAD 257

A7 IS IT POSSIBLE TO FALL FROM GRACE? 264

A8 WHAT DO THE WORDS *WATER AND THE SPIRIT* IN JOHN 3:5 MEAN? 275

BIBLIOGRAPHY 285

RECOMMENDED BOOKS FOR ADDITIONAL STUDY 295

Edward James Wittlif

INTRODUCTION

There are many great books on baptism and salvation, so why another? The lack of unity among Christians is the reason for this book. This lack should be a major concern for all believers. It must cause great sadness to our Lord and Savior, who prayed for unity among His followers the night He was betrayed as recorded in John 17. However, unity cannot not be based on what man thinks. As Jesus said, *"Enter through the narrow gate, for the gate is wide and the way is broad that leads to destruction, and there are many who enter through it. For the gate is small and the way is narrow that leads to life, and there are few who find it"* (Matthew 7:13-14).

Baptism is a misunderstood and misused term. Some see it as a work of man; others as a work of God. Baptism is seen as essential to putting on Christ and being raised to a new life by one group, while another views it as an unnecessary rite. Different groups administer it by immersion, sprinkling, pouring, or only with the Spirit. Some baptize infants, while others baptize based on the age of accountability. That is the age when a person knows he has sin and knows he needs a Savior. Baptism is ignored by many who just use a simple prayer asking Jesus into their hearts. Baptism is also viewed only as a public affirmation that one is already saved. Others believe it is just a step in joining a local church.

BAPTISM WHAT IS IT GOOD FOR?

Is there a clear-cut answer in the Scriptures concerning baptism and its purpose or place and the means of doing it? After all, God is not a God of confusion (I Corinthians 14:33). Therefore, it would seem we should be able to understand what God means about baptism. God has not given us the Scriptures to confuse us. He has given us His word so that we have what we need to know in order to restore the relationship with Him that was lost in the Garden and by our own choices ever since.

Why is it important to understand baptism? Jesus told the apostles that He has total authority both in heaven and on earth. He then gave them this order: *"Go therefore and make disciples of all the nations, baptizing them in the name of the Father and the Son and the Holy Spirit, teaching them to observe all that I commanded you"* (Matthew 28:18-20). *"He said to them, 'Go into all the world and preach the good news to all creation. Whoever believes and is baptized will be saved, but whoever does not believe will be condemned"* (Mark 16:15-16 NIV).

Jesus orders that believers be baptized, and He has been given the authority to issue commands. Baptism is therefore mandatory. The Lord prayed for unity among His followers, and yet His followers are split over many things, especially baptism.

We must seek to understand what is true with an open mind. A problem to face as we go through this study is that we all have a traditionalistic view based on whatever Christian group we belong to, which influences the way we view the Scriptures. We need to set aside our traditional viewpoints and read the Scriptures with an open mind. Remember that the chapters and verse numbers were put in by man and not God. Therefore, as we read the word of God, we need to read the context rather than just a verse.

The Scriptures were written to be understood. *"All Scripture is inspired by God and profitable for teaching, for reproof, for correction, for training in righteousness; so that the man of God may be adequate, equipped for every good work"* (II Timothy 3:16-17). Therefore, we should be able to understand it as written. To gain an understanding of the Bible should not be difficult if we read it carefully. God communicates in a clear, understanding way in matters of what He expects of us and what He wants us to know. There are parts of the Bible that are hard to understand, but these are prophetic. However, when it comes to living a godly life and salvation, those parts are understandable. If we cannot understand a book, it is a waste of time and effort to read it.

Fighting over words leads to the destruction of unity. This usually manifests itself in adding meanings or words that do not exist in God's word. An example would be if I say, "Eve gave Adam an apple." You say no, "It was a pear." Another says, "You are both wrong. It was a peach." We all dig our heels in and wind up with three totally separate churches. Consider what Paul wrote to Timothy, *"Keep reminding them of these things. Warn them before God against quarreling about words; it is of no value, and only ruins those who listen"* (II Timothy 2:14 NIV).

BAPTISM WHAT IS IT GOOD FOR?

When one teaches traditions or what a confident-sounding person says or writes, hearers often fail to read the Word of God with an open mind. Rather than follow what the apostle said, the Bereans examined the Scriptures daily to be certain for themselves as to what Paul was teaching (Acts 17:11).

Therefore, as I write this book examining baptism, I will strive to approach this important subject with an open mind attentive to what God has said. I encourage those who read this work to read it with an open mind and seek a clear understanding of the purpose and meaning of baptism through the scriptures.

As you read this book, know there is nothing that anyone can do that will earn him eternal life. *"... the free gift of God is eternal life in Christ Jesus our Lord"* (Romans 6:23b). As Paul wrote, *"I do not nullify the grace of God, for if righteousness comes through the Law, then Christ died needlessly"* (Galatians 2:21). In Ephesians we are told, *"For by grace you have been saved through faith; and that not of yourselves, it is the gift of God; not as a result of works, so that no one may boast"* (Ephesians 2:8-9). Neither Law keeping nor any amount of works will earn anyone salvation because if we could earn salvation, then Christ Jesus' sacrifice is pointless. We are saved by grace, not works.

We need to examine all the passages in the writings of the apostles and the other men who were chosen to write the books of the New Testament regarding baptism. We will be seeking to discover what is accomplished by being baptized, our part, God's part, and if we can determine if baptism is really tied to salvation.

There are several things connected with acquiring eternal life or salvation in the scriptures. These are beyond just belief and baptism. Baptism is but one part that must be examined. Many other things connected scripturally with salvation are examined and included in this book.

Consider the following from Ephesians Chapter Four as you go through this book:

> *4:1 Therefore I, the prisoner of the Lord, implore you to walk in a manner worthy of the calling with which you have been called, 2 with all humility and gentleness, with patience, showing tolerance for one another in love, 3 being diligent to preserve the unity of the Spirit in the bond of peace. 4 There is one body and one Spirit, just as also you were called in one hope of your calling; 5 one Lord, one faith, one baptism, 6 one God and Father of all who is over all and through all and in all* (Ephesians 4:1-6).

Jesus prayed for unity among His followers. The Holy Spirit through Paul calls for us to preserve the unity in the bond of peace. The lack of unity must cause great pain and sorrow to the Father, Son, and Holy Spirit.

Consider that body, Spirit, hope, Lord, faith, baptism, and God the Father are all singular, not plural.

BAPTISM WHAT IS IT GOOD FOR?

We need to understand that God desires two things. *"Who desires all people to be saved and to come to the knowledge of the truth"* (I Timothy 2:4 ESV). God wants everyone to be saved and to learn the truth. The purpose of this book is not to ram a doctrine down the reader's throat. The purpose is to cause all of us to examine God's word in regard to truly having a restored relationship with Him.

I ask as you read this book you pray for an open mind free of traditions as I have striven to do in writing this book. Keeping this principle in mind, let us examine the things God includes in our salvation.

CHAPTER ONE
WHAT IS NECESSARY FOR SALVATION?

The question that we must have an answer to is what does God consider necessary for salvation?

We need to look through God's word to see if there is a pattern. Can we see if God has clearly revealed what is involved in being redeemed or saved? Or is it up to each individual or group to make his or their own way? Remember that Jesus said, *"For the gate is small and the way is narrow that leads to life, and there are few who find it"* (Matthew 7:14). In the preceding verse Jesus said, *"Enter through the narrow gate; for the gate is wide and the way is broad that leads to destruction, and there are many who enter through it"* (Matthew 7:13).

Two gates — a wide open one that is easy to find and enter through, but it leads to destruction, not life. The second gate is narrow, and few actually find it. *"You will seek Me and find Me when you search for Me with all your heart"* (Jeremiah 29:13). That verse implies a strong desire to find God and a deep hunger for knowing God. Hebrews 11:6 states that if we seek God, He will reward us. To find that narrow gate we need to want it more than anything else in the world.

In Jesus' discussion of the Good Shepherd and the door He spoke of entrance into the sheep fold. *"I am the door; if anyone enters through Me, he will be saved, and will go in and out and find pasture"* (John 10:9). To be saved one must enter through Jesus. Therefore, we see that entrance through the gate into life must be through Jesus (Matthew 7:14 and John 5:21-23).

These are powerful words concerning salvation: *"Salvation is found in no one else, for there is no other name under heaven given to men by which we must be saved"* (Acts 4:12 NIV). Salvation cannot be found in anyone other than in Jesus. God will not recognize any other name or person as savior.

Gareth L. Reese says about Acts 4:12:

> Such salvation, including the forgiveness of sin and the opportunity for eternal life with God in heaven, says Peter, is available in no one else save Jesus Christ of Nazareth. There is salvation in no other person — only in Jesus. There is emphasis upon the negative, which in the Greek stands in the very first part of the sentence. There is NO chance. There is NO other way.[1]

Reese continues:

> All of us must be saved by faith and obedience to Christ if we are going to be saved at all! "Must" does not imply the necessity of salvation, as though everybody just had to be saved (they have no choice in the matter). Rather, this implies the necessity of having Christ if we are to have salvation. If you are going to be saved, you will have to come the way Jesus instructed. Similarly,

in Romans 1-3, Paul shows the failure of all other ways. He points up the fact that salvation is only through faith in Christ.[2]

Acts 4:12 makes it clear God will not save anyone who comes to Him through any other way than Jesus.

Acts 4:12 fits with Jesus's words, *"I am the way, and the truth, and the life; no one comes to the Father but through Me"* (John 14:6b). Jesus is the only way to God, the Father. To be saved we must come through Jesus, for only He is the only way and the only door.

In John 6:60-66 we learn that Jesus' words were hard and many disciples left Him. Jesus asked the twelve, *"Do you want to go away as well?"* (John 6:67b ESV) *"Simon Peter answered him, 'Lord, to whom shall we go? You the words of eternal life"* (John 6:68 ESV). Peter and the others knew that Jesus was the promised one of God by the miracles He had done and His words. No one else can deliver on the promise of eternal life. The author of Hebrews tells us, *"In the past God spoke to our forefathers through the prophets at many times and in various ways, but in these last days he has spoken to us by his Son"* (Hebrews 1:1-2a NIV). The final word has come through Jesus. This is more than just the words that are colored red in Bibles.

Heed what Jesus told the disciples the night He was betrayed. *"I have much more to tell you, more than you can now bear. But when he, the Spirit of truth comes, he will guide you into all truth. He will not speak on his own, he will speak only what he hears"* (John 16:12-13a NIV). All the words in the Bible are from God through the Word (John 1:1). If you want to hear the words of eternal life, then read the Holy Word.

Since the way is narrow and is only through Jesus, we need to see what is required to enter through Jesus. What does Jesus say about how we are saved?

CHAPTER ONE: WHAT IS NECESSARY FOR SALVATION?

1. Gareth L. Reese, *New Testament History Acts,* by College Press: Joplin, Missouri, 1983, pages 179-180.
2. ibid, page 180.

CHAPTER TWO:
SAVED BY GRACE

"For by grace you have been saved" (Ephesians 2:8a).

Grace is what a loving God gives freely to totally undeserving people. Through grace our sins are forgiven. Through grace we have a restored relationship with our heavenly Father. Through grace we have the hope of eternal life with God. The offer of salvation is universal. *"He* (Jesus) *is the atoning sacrifice for our sins, and not only for ours but also for the sins of the whole world"* (I John 2:2 NIV).

Does grace mean that God will automatically forgive the sins of every single person who ever lived? Read carefully the words that the apostle John was told to write, *"Blessed are those who wash their robes, so they have the right to the tree of life, and may enter by the gates into the city. Outside are the dogs and the sorcerers and the immoral persons and the murders and the idolaters, and everyone who loves and practices lying"* (Revelation 22:14-15). The grace of God, although offered freely for everyone universally, will not be applied universally. If everyone were saved by grace, then Revelation 22:14-15 is a lie. If grace is applied universally, then all listed there will be saved no matter what their sin is and certainly against their will. To be honest, if we are all saved by grace, what are we doing here on earth and going through all the things that harm us? If God is going to save everyone, why didn't He just put us in heaven?

In the beginning chapters of the letter to the Romans the point is made that, Jew or Gentle, all are sinners, *"For all have sinned and fall short of the glory of God, being justified as a gift by His grace through the redemption which is Christ Jesus"* (Romans 3:23-24). Everyone needs God's grace because we have all sinned against God. *"But where sin increased, grace abounded all the more"* (Romans 5:20b). Following that, we read in Chapter Six: *"What shall we say, then? Shall we go on sinning so that grace may increase? By no means! We died to sin, how can we live in it any longer?"* (Romans 6:1-2 NIV). Therefore, a change of lifestyle is expected in those who have accepted God's offer of grace.

> *In the same way, count yourselves dead to sin but alive to God in Christ Jesus. Therefore do not let sin reign in your mortal body so that you obey its evil desires. Do not offer the parts of your body to sin, as instruments of wickedness, but rather offer yourselves to God, as those who have been brought from death to life; and offer the parts of your body to him as instruments of righteousness. For sin shall not be your master, because you are not under law, but under grace* (Romans 6:11-14 NIV).

When we come to Christ Jesus and accept God's free offer of grace, our past sins are removed and not remembered by God. We should out of gratitude and love strive to be what God desires us to be.

BAPTISM WHAT IS IT GOOD FOR?

God desires us to be holy. *"Therefore, prepare your minds for action; be self-controlled; set your hope fully on the grace to be given to you when Jesus Christ is revealed. As obedient children, do not conform to the evil desires you had when you lived in ignorance. But just as he who called you is holy, so be holy in all you do; for it is written: 'Be holy, because I am holy'"* (I Peter 1:13-16 NIV). God desires this for every single person.

We read in I Timothy 2:4 that God our savior *"... desires all men to be saved and to come to the knowledge of the truth."* God desires two things in that verse; 1. He wants all men to be saved. 2. He wants all men to learn the truth. Our heavenly Father loves us so much He is unwilling to abandon us and cast us away. He has through His word revealed the truth, that sin has separated us from Him and that the Son of God came down as one of us and paid the redemptive price reuniting us with God.

Isaiah speaks of God's love and willingness to forgive us. *"Come now, and let us reason together', Says the Lord, "Though your sins are as scarlet, they will be as white as snow; though they are like crimson, they will be like wool. If you consent and obey'"* (Isaiah 1:18-19a). The rest of verse 19 gives a promise that is followed in verse 20 with a warning. It is not a reasoning together with God on what to do. God has already determined what is to be done. They are sinners, and only grace can wipe away sin. God's grace, while freely given, is always based on the recipient's acceptance and obedience.

In his commentary on Isaiah, F. Delitzschs refers to Isaiah 1:18 as a trial, one in which Israel stands condemned based on how they responded to the verses before:

> Yet Jehovah will not treat Israel according to His retributive justice, but according to His free compassion. He will remit the punishment, and not only regard the sin as not existing, but change it into its very opposite. The reddest possible sin shall become, through His mercy, the purest white....It is a deeply significant symbol of the act of justification. Jehovah offers to Israel an *actio forensic*, out of which it shall come forth justified by grace, although it has merited death on account of its sins. The righteousness, white as snow and wool, with which Israel comes forth is a gift conferred upon it out of pure compassion, without being conditional upon any legal performance whatever.[1]

In his comments on verses 19-20, F. Delitzsch says; "But after the restoration of Israel *in integrum* by this act of grace, the rest would unquestionably depend upon the conduct of Israel itself. According to Israel's own decision would Jehovah determine Israel's future."[2]

Grace covers sins that we aren't even aware that we committed and those that we were unable to repent of before becoming either incapacitated or dead. The bottom line for a Christian is to live a life that is Spirit led.

BAPTISM WHAT IS IT GOOD FOR?

How does grace fit in with salvation and eternal life with God? Salvation is the offer of God given freely. Grace is based entirely upon God's love and the sacrifice of His only begotten Son. Grace is available only because the Son of God freely paid the redemption price fully for every single person. In fact, without grace there would be no salvation. Grace has to be connected to faith. Faith involves belief and trust. *"And without faith it is impossible to please Him, for he who comes to God must believe that He is and that He is a rewarder of those who seek Him"* (Hebrews 11:6). This verse connects belief in God with a trust that God will keep His word and do what He promises to do.

Grace is universally offered to all. Grace has to be available to every single person because *"For there is no partiality with God"* (Romans 2:11 and Acts 10:34). However, does God force grace on anyone? If grace is given to all, every single person, from people like Hitler to Mother Teresa, will have to be saved. People will then be saved without even repenting. In fact, they can be liars, commit murder, abuse children, torture people, etc. and not even feel sorry for their actions and be with God throughout eternity. That would make God a liar, according to verses like Revelation 22:15.

We need to understand that God's holiness and righteousness and purity demand the same characteristics in humanity since He created us in His image. *"This is the message we have heard from Him and announce to you, that God is Light, and in Him there is no darkness at all. If we say that we have fellowship with Him and yet walk in the darkness, we lie and do not practice the truth; but if we walk in the Light as He Himself is in the Light. We have fellowship with one another, and the blood of Jesus His Son cleanses us from all sin"* (I John 1:5-7). *"As obedient children, do not be conformed to the former lusts which were yours in your ignorance, but like the Holy One who called you, be holy yourselves also in all your behavior"* (I Peter 1:14-15).

There is no darkness or evil nature in God; therefore, to be with Him for eternity we must be holy and pure. God's integrity is consistent and unchanging, He cannot sweep sin under the carpet, as it were, and ignore it. God must deal with sin.

While grace is offered to all, there are conditions to be met, as I trust we will see from God's word.

The concept "conditions to be met" is widely misunderstood. Many mistakenly think if I must meet conditions or do something, I must earn God's grace. When I receive God's grace, something happens which affects my reaction after receiving grace. If I understand what God's grace means for me and what it cost God, I should respond in a manner corresponding to the value of grace. Do I understand I was separated from God and I was His enemy, and I was hopelessly condemned? If I do, then grace is worth more than all the world has to offer, and I will be moved to give my life to Jesus because He gave His life for me. Paul said it this way: *"I have been crucified with Christ; and it is no longer I who live, but Christ lives in me; and the life which I now live in the flesh I live by faith in the Son of God, who loved me and gave Himself up for me"* (Galatians 2:20). What is involved in Christ living in us is a new mindset and a changing life.

When I understand that God loves me so much that He asked His Son to take my justly earned wrath and punishment upon Himself, I will give myself unconditionally to Him. That means that I now live my life governed by Jesus and not myself.

Before we move on, we need to look at how God, a righteous, just, and holy God can offer grace to sinners.

What Is The Basis for God's Grace?

Did God just decide that since we sinned, He was going to forgive us and ignore our sins? This is the view of people who tend to see God as only love. They limit God to only one characteristic of His nature, which is love. Therefore, because if God is only love, then when we disobey Him and sin, He automatically forgives us. That view is a narrow view of what love is. Godly love is wanting the best for others, and that includes discipline or tough love. The God who only loves people also embrace the idea that God will save all good people, no matter which god they believe in or even if they do not believe in any god. The problem is when we put God in a box, we ignore who God is. He is love, just, wrathful, holy, sinless, and righteous to the point that He hates sin. He cannot sweep sin under the carpet. Sin must be dealt with.

"But surely good people are okay." That is really what many teach and believe. However, Jesus dealt with that idea, *"As Jesus started on his way, a man ran up to him and fell on his knees before him. 'Good teacher,' he asked, 'what must I do to inherit eternal life?' 'Why do you call me good?' Jesus answered. 'No one is good — except God alone"* (Mark 10:17-18 NIV). Jesus set God as the standard for being good. Note that the man asked, *"What must I do?"* Jesus answered that you cannot be good enough to earn or deserve eternal life because the standard of being good is God.

"This is the message we have heard from him and declare to you: God is light; in him there is no darkness at all" (I John 1:5 NIV). There is no evil and no sin in God at all. To be totally good is the standard. Anyone who falls even just barely short of that removes his being considered good. Every one of us is not good. *"For all have sinned and fall short of the glory of God"* (Romans 3:23 NIV). There isn't a one of us who doesn't need God's grace.

Creation includes man and woman. *"God saw all that He had made, and behold, **it was very good"*** (Genesis 1:31a). Adam and Eve had a personal relationship with God demonstrated by the fact that God walked in the garden with them (Genesis 3:8). Mankind was without sin. God gave Adam and Eve one very simple restriction. They were forbidden to eat of one tree out of all the trees in Eden (Genesis 2:16, 17). Failure to restrain themselves from eating the fruit of that one tree would result in death. The death penalty would be carried out the very same day. God, to create humanity in His image, had to give us the ability to choose. In doing so, God had to place a choice for us to make. That choice was to obey or not.

Adam and Eve sinned by breaking the one commandment God gave them and thus came under the penalty (Genesis 3:6-24). God cursed mankind with hard work and physical death, *"By the sweat of your face you will eat bread, till you return to the ground, because from it you were taken; for you are dust, and to dust you shall return"* (Genesis 3:19). God also drove them out of the garden so they could not eat of the tree of life (Genesis 3:24). Not only did this prevent them from eating of the tree of life, but they no longer had an intimate walk with God. They were now physically separated from the presence of God. Death as separation came the very same day. Physical death, separation of body and soul came later. I believe that is because God allows time for us to come to our senses and return to Him.

Nelson Smith wrote concerning sin:

> Sin immediately alienates us from God, separates us from Him! Again, let the prophet Isaiah tell us: "Behold the Lord's hand is not shortened, that it cannot save; neither his ear heavy, that it cannot hear: But your sins have hid his face from you, that he will not hear" (Isaiah 59:1,2). Notice it is "your sins" that have "<u>separated</u>" man from God. This separated condition Paul calls death. "And you hath he quickened (made alive) who were dead in

> trespasses and sins" (Ephesians 1:1). And incidentally, separation is what death is. In physical death the spirit or soul is separated from the body (Genesis 35:18; James 2:26). In being dead to sin man is separated from God (Isaiah 59:1,2) .... And, finally, the second death is separation from God eternally (Revelation 20:11-15; II Thessalonians 1:8,9[3]

Because of our sins we are separated from God. *"God is Light, and in Him there is no darkness at all"* (I John 1:5b). What does it mean that God is Light?

Lanier, Jr. wrote:

> Notice God is not said to be "a light," but **light itself.** He is perfectly pure with no blots, stains, errors, mistakes, or sins ... He is perfectly righteous, with nothing unholy or impure. ... **In him is no darkness at all —** John now states the negative for the sake of emphasis.
>
> Not even one small shadow, absolutely nothing is ever present to blot or dim God's light. "Darkness" (SKOTIA) is often used to indicate evil. "...delivered us out of darkness ..." (Ephesians 6:12)[4]

God is one hundred percent good, righteous, honest, trustworthy, dependable, faithful, unchanging, and the list goes on. There is no sin in God. There are aspects of the very character of God that govern His ability to give sinners grace.

God's Characteristics Governing Grace in Order That He Can Stay God

Holiness. Roy Lanier, Sr., quotes Hodge as defining holiness. "Holiness, on the one hand, implies entire freedom from moral evil; and, upon the other, absolute moral perfection. Freedom from impurity is the primary idea of the word. To sanctify is to cleanse; to be holy, is to be clean."[5]

Lanier, Sr., writes, "We have defined holiness in God as that essential element in his nature which causes him to hate, with perfect hatred, everything that is morally evil, and to love everything that is pure and holy."[6]

Peter tells us that God's people must, *"As obedient children, do not be conformed to the former lusts which were yours in ignorance, but like the Holy One who called you, be holy yourselves also in all your behavior; because it is written, 'You shall be holy, for I am holy"* (I Peter 1:14-16).

God hates sin because He is holy and He desires us to match His holiness. His holiness forces Him to deal with sin. Hence, *"The soul who sins will die"* (Ezekiel 18:4c). The soul that dies in its sins will be separated from God. Does this give God pleasure? *'Do I have any pleasure in the death of the wicked,' declares the Lord God, "rather than that he should turn from his ways and live"* (Ezekiel

18:23). Unless the sinner turns to God, he has no hope. *"God desires all men to be saved"* (I Timothy 2:4). The loving God has done and is doing everything to prevent anyone from going to hell. The problem is some refuse to believe, while others refuse to be obedient. Therefore, they condemn themselves. God does not condemn anyone, and He does not send anyone to Hell. The one who rejects God is the one who condemns himself and joins with the devil and his angels.

There is one thing we need to understand. While God hates sin, He still loves sinners and wants them to be reconciled to Him. If God hated sinners, He never would have made provision for their salvation. Therefore, Christians must also hate sin, but love sinners.

Lanier, Sr. quotes Conner regarding God's righteousness. "God's righteousness condemns sin in man. This is punitive righteousness. Man, universally falls short of the standard as set by a righteous God ... As a righteous God he must condemn man's sin ... he would not be righteous if he did not condemn it."[7]

The righteousness of God is the very standard of our being righteous. It is a high bar to attain to. The standard requires that we always do what is right. In Romans, Paul wrote that there is no difference between Jew and Gentile as both have fallen short of the glory of God. "But now apart from the Law the righteousness of God has been manifested, being witnessed by the Law and the Prophets, even the righteousness of God through faith in Christ Jesus for all those who believe for there is no distinction; for all have sinned and fall short of the glory of God" (Romans 3:21-23).

McGarvey comments, "It is bestowed upon Jew and Gentile without distinction, for both classes, having failed to attain that perfection of righteousness which is the glory of God, are equally condemned without it."[8]

We are reminded that sinning earns us death (Romans 6:23). Also, *"Or do you not know that the unrighteous will not inherit the kingdom of God?"* (I Corinthians 6:9a). No one who is unrighteous will enter heaven (Revelation 21:27).

Vine gives this definition of *just*: "Said of God, it designates the perfect agreement between His nature and His acts (in which He is the standard for all men)."[9]

Lanier, Sr., quotes from Watson:

> Watson, in his **Theological Institutes,** defines justice as follows: Justice in its principle, is holiness, and is often expressed by the term "righteousness"; but when it relates to matters of government, the universal rectitude of the divine nature shows itself in inflexible regard to what is **right,** and in opposition to **wrong,** which cannot be warped or altered in any degree.[10]

God's holiness, righteousness, and His being just say that He cannot turn a blind eye and ignore our sins. Therefore,

God cannot just forgive us and remain true to His nature. Sin is disobedience to God and His commandments; it is a rejection of God as our Lord. When we sin, it is an act of rebellion against our Creator by making ourselves god. We must understand that sin is deadly serious with eternal consequences. Sin separates us from a relationship with God. God promised that if Adam and Eve disobeyed Him and ate of the tree of the knowledge of good and evil, they would die. Death is a separation. Thus, their relationship with God was severed.

God's dilemma is that He desires a relationship with mankind, but He cannot ignore our disobedience. The penalty must be paid because God cannot overlook disobedience. The penalty is separation from God. Remember that I John 1:5 says that God is Light. Jesus calls separation as being cast *"out into the outer darkness"* (Matthew 8:12, 22:13, 25:30, and Luke 13:28). There is no mention of the sentence of separation having a time limit. How does God resolve it so that He can extend an offer of grace?

Emmanuel, God with Us, Came Down to Die for Us; And That Is How God Can Grant Grace

Jesus said, *"the Son of Man did not come to be served, but to serve, and to give His life a ransom for many"* (Matthew 20:28). Emmanuel left heaven, lived among us (John 1:14), became one of us (Hebrews 2:17), and was tempted like us and yet without sin (Hebrews 4:15).

BAPTISM WHAT IS IT GOOD FOR?

Lanier, Sr., stated:

> The justice of God made the atonement necessary when man sinned. Sin is a violation of God's law; which law is made necessary by the very nature of God. The penalty for violation of God's law is death and separation from God. This penalty had to be suffered. But if man suffered it, he would be eternally destroyed from God. Jesus died in man's place to satisfy the justice of God and make it possible for God to forgive man of sin and live eternally with God. Justice, the transitive holiness of God, demanded death as the penalty for man's sin; mercy, the transitive love of God, furnished a substitute for man in the person of Jesus Christ, the Son of God, so God could be righteous and man could be saved.[11]

Emmanuel, God with us, stepped in and took the Godhead's wrath upon Himself in order that the penalty could be satisfied. What unbelievable love from man's viewpoint!

Peter wrote, *"... you were not redeemed with perishable things like silver or gold from your futile way of life inherited from your forefathers, but with precious blood, as of a lamb unblemished and spotless, the blood of Christ"* (I Peter 1:18-19). We read in Revelation 1:5 that Jesus *"loves us and released us from our sins by His blood."*

God made Jesus, who was sinless, sin for us in order for us to be righteous before God (II Corinthians 5:21). About seven hundred years earlier, God spoke these words through Isaiah: *"But He was pierced through for our transgressions, He was crushed for our iniquities; the chastening for our well-being fell upon Him, and by His scourging we are healed. All of us like sheep have gone astray, each of us has turned to his own way; but the Lord has caused the iniquity of us all to fall on Him"* (Isaiah 53:5-6).

Jesus, Emmanuel, Son of Man, Son of God, God's Anointed Messiah, Creator, maintainer of the universe, willingly went to the cross taking upon Himself our justly earned and deserved punishment. Jesus the Christ stood in our place. He did this when we had no hope and no way out.

God loves us so much that even while we were sinners and enemies of His, He demonstrated His love by having His only begotten Son die for each and every one of us (Romans 5:6-11 and John 3:16).

That is why God can stay holy, righteous, and just while offering us grace. He offered a suitable substitute in our place. The only acceptable sacrifice is someone who could sin and yet never committed one sin. Paul said it this way, *"He made Him who knew no sin to be sin on our behalf, so that we might become the righteousness of God in Him"* (II Corinthians 5:21). Speaking of Jesus John wrote, *"And*

BAPTISM WHAT IS IT GOOD FOR?

He Himself is the propitiation for our sins; and not for ours only, but also for those of the whole world" (I John 2:2).

Roy Lanier, Jr., in his *Epistles of John* states:

> God's perfect hatred of sin. It is not petty irritability, or arbitrary anger. This anger calling for propitiation, may be perfectly justified. The moral governance of the universe is at stake, as it demands justice and wrath for those who violate God's laws. Remembering that "sin is transgression of God's law," and "lawlessness" (I John 3:4), one can understand that God's consistency would inevitably call for punishment of those who thus violate His law.[12]

Barnes points out four important things regarding propitiation that we need to understand:

> (1,) that his will has been disregarded, and his law violated, and that he has reason to be offended with us; (2,) that in that condition he cannot, consistently with his perfections, and the good of the universe, treat us as if we had not done it; (3,) that it is proper that, in some way, he should show his displeasure at our conduct, either by punishing us, or by something that shall answer the same purpose; and, (4,) that the means of propitiation comes in here, and accomplish this end, and make it proper that he should treat us as if we had not

sinned; that is, he is reconciled, or appeased, and his anger is turned away. This is done, it is supposed, by the death of the Lord Jesus, accomplishing, in most important respects, what would be accomplished by the punishment of the offender himself.[13]

Consider these verses:

> *But now a righteousness from God, apart from law, has been made known, to which the Law and the Prophets testify. This righteousness from God comes through faith in Jesus Christ to all who believe. There is no difference, for all have sinned and fall short of the glory of God, and are justified freely by his grace through the redemption that came by Christ Jesus. God presented him as a sacrifice of atonement, through faith in his blood. He did this to demonstrate his justice, because in his forbearance he had left the sins committed beforehand unpunished — he did it to demonstration his justice at the present time, so as to be just and the one who justifies those who have faith in Jesus* (Romans 3:21-26 NIV).

God's plan from even before the beginning was to take on our sins and punishment on Himself through the member of the Godhead who became like us. Thus, looking ahead, God was able to overlook the sins of those who were obedient to Him before the cross.

F.F. Bruce comments on Romans 3:21:

BAPTISM WHAT IS IT GOOD FOR?

> But now a new way to acceptance with God has been opened up, a completely different way from that of legal obedience. Yet this is no new-fangled way, thought up by ourselves; it has ample witness borne to it in advance in the Old Testament writings — in the Law and the Prophets.[14]

Peter tells us God planned the sacrifice of His Son before creation. *"For you know that it was not with perishable things such as silver or gold that you were redeemed from the empty way of life handed down to you from your forefathers, but with the precious blood of Christ, a lamb without blemish or defect, He was chosen before the creation of the world"* (I Peter 1:18-20a, NIV). The Godhead knew even before anything was created what must be done. It amazes me that God, knowing what we would do and the cost to Him to redeem us, went ahead and created us anyway. In this I see my value to my Creator, Father, and God. Because of the worth God placed on me, I love and honor my God and my Savior.

God passed over the sins committed before the sacrifice of His Son. In comparing the effectiveness of the animal sacrifices offered under the Law with Jesus Christ's sacrifice, we read in Hebrews, *"For it is impossible for the blood of bulls and goats to take away sins"* (Hebrews 10:4). Animals cannot be an equal sacrifice with a man because animals are not capable of sinning or living a holy and righteous life. For all those who died prior to the cross, their sins were remembered. The people were not made perfect by the yearly animal sacrifices (Hebrews 10:1).

What has removed the sins of obedient believers was the offering one time of the body of Jesus Christ (Hebrews 10:10). Jesus left heaven and His glory to become just like us (Philippians 2:6-8 and Hebrews 2:17-18). He was tempted, but never sinned. Therefore, He could stand in for us and satisfy God's justice.

God's ability to forgive every obedient believer, past, present, and future, depends totally on Jesus' atoning sacrifice. The animal sacrifices demonstrated the need for death to satisfy God's wrath against sin, pointing ahead to Christ's sacrifice. Making of the animal sacrifices for sin prior to the cross required three things of the believer — the acknowledgement of sin, obedience to God's commands to sacrifice a perfect animal, and a trust in God's promise of cleansing. The atoning sacrifice of God's only begotten Son satisfied God's justice for all obedient faithful believers

reaching back to Adam and forward to the return of Jesus. *"And for this reason He is the mediator of a new covenant, in order that since a death has taken place for the redemption of the transgressions that were committed under the first covenant, those who have been called may receive the promise of the eternal inheritance"* (Hebrews 9:15).

"And their sins and their lawless deeds I will remember no more" (Hebrews 10:17). The atoning sacrifice of Jesus Christ, the only begotten Son of God, enables God to

forgive and forget our sins. God can now do this and remain one hundred percent faithful to His nature.

We are told that all sins are lawlessness and against God, but we are warned especially of sexual immorality. *"Flee from sexual immorality. All other sins a man commits are outside his body, but he who sins sexually sins against his own body. Do you not know that your body is a temple of the Holy Spirit, who is in you, whom you have received from God? You are not your own: you were bought at a price. Therefore honor God with your body"* (I Corinthians 6:18-20 NIV). That price was the life of the Son of God.

"Therefore there is now no condemnation for those who are in Christ Jesus" (Romans 8:1). Only when we are in Christ can we stand uncondemned and righteous before Almighty God.

CHAPTER TWO: SAVED BY GRACE

1. F. Delitzsch, *Volume 7 Isaiah, Commentary On The Old Testament,* by C.F. Keil and F. Delitzsch, Translated by James Martin, Hendrickson Publishers, March 2006, pages 64-65.
2. Ibid page 65.
3. Nelson Smith, *An Analysis of Sin,* Western Christian Foundation, P.O. Drawer W, Wichita Falls, Texas 76308, page 27.
4. Roy H. Lanier, Jr., *Epistles of John, Notes on 1,2,3 John,* Quality Publications, P.O. Box 1060, Abilene, Texas, 79604-1060, 1992, pages 12, 13.
5. Roy H. Lanier, Sr., *The Timeless Trinity for the Ceaseless Centuries,* Published by Roy H. Lanier, Sr., Denver, Colorado. 1974. Page 93.
6. Ibid, Page 99.
7. Ibid, Page 110.
8. J.W. McGarvey, and Philip Y. Pendleton, *Thessalonians, Corinthians, Galatians, and Romans, The Standard Bible Commentary,* The Standard Publishing Foundation, Cincinnati, Ohio, page 321.
9. W.E. Vine, Merrill F. Unger, William White, Jr., *Vine's Expository Dictionary of Biblical Words,* Thomas Nelson Publishers, Nashville, Camden, New York, 1985, page 338.
10. Lanier, Sr., page 106.
11. Ibid, pages 116-117.
12. Lanier, Jr., page 26.

13. Albert Barnes, *Barnes' Notes on the New Testament,* edited by Ingram Cobbin, Complete and Unabridged In One Volume, Kregel Publications, Grand Rapids, Michigan, 1975, page 1471.
14. F.F. Bruce, *The Epistle of Paul To The Romans An Introduction and Commentary,* Wm. B. Eerdmans Publishing Company, Grand Rapids, Michigan, 1969, page 99.

CHAPTER THREE:
THE OLD COVENANT VERSUS THE NEW COVENANT

To understand salvation in Christ, we need to see the difference between the Old Covenant and the New Covenant. Consider, *"Therefore the Law has become our tutor to lead us to Christ, so that we may be justified by faith"* (Galatians 3:24). The Law or the Old Covenant taught that keeping law on your own is impossible and that breaking the Law condemns. In Hebrews we learn that animal sacrifices cannot remove sins and that there was a constant reminder because they had to continue to offer sacrifices. (Hebrews 10:1-4). All this served to teach a need for a Savior and drive home the point that sins must be paid for.

Actually, we need to begin with Abraham, the father of the faithful. When Abraham was ninety-nine years old God instituted circumcision as a sign of the covenant He had made with Abraham (Genesis 17:9-27). Circumcision passed on to Abraham's descendants as a sign of covenant relationship with God. Circumcision continued under the Law given through Moses (Exodus 12:43-49 and Leviticus 12:3). Under the New Covenant circumcision still is a sign of covenant relationship. Believers are now circumcised by Christ (Colossians 2:11).

Circumcision of male babies at eight days old was required under the Law given through Moses (Leviticus 12:3). The first-born that opened the womb belonged to God and was set apart to God (Exodus 13:1). The first-born male was to be redeemed (Exodus 13:13).

God required a sign that they were covenant related from eight days forward. If a male was uncircumcised, he was not covenant related to God. In the New Covenant all believers, male and female, are circumcised not by a physical act, but a spiritual act. *"And in Him you were also circumcised with a circumcision made without hands, in the removal of the body of flesh by the circumcision of Christ"* (Colossians 2:11).

Jesus, born under the Law, was no exception. On the eighth day after birth, He was brought to Jerusalem and presented to God, named, circumcised, and the appropriate sacrifice offered for redeeming the first male child (Luke 2:21-24).

As the children grew up under the Old Law, they were to be taught about God and the covenant that they were part of. They had no idea what they were part of until they were taught and old enough to understand.

The Holy Spirit contrasts the first covenant with the second in Hebrews chapter 8 beginning with verse 7. The first covenant was a covenant of law or rule keeping. When you are under a system of rules, you must keep them perfectly. When you break any single law or rule, you have to pay the penalty. The first covenant had through the system of yearly sacrifices a constant reminder of sin and its guilt (Hebrews 10:3). As Hebrews 8:7 says, the first covenant was with faults. A covenant based on law or rule keeping can only punish and not wipe the slate clean until the price for breaking the law is met.

The author of Hebrews quoted Jeremiah 31:31 in which God promised a new covenant to replace the faulty one. The old covenant served its purpose. It taught us that law or rule keeping will not work for one huge reason. The reason was if you break one rule, you must pay the penalty. *"The person who sins will die..."* (Ezekiel 18:20a). The penalty is not just physical death but eternal separation from God. That God never intended that the old covenant would be the final one is made clear in Galatians and Hebrews.

Under the Law babies were born covenant related. They then had to be taught about God and their relationship to Him. They learned about sin and sacrifice. The contrast between the old and the new covenants is that under the first, those physically born into a Jewish family were in covenant with God. It was a covenant made with the chosen people, the physical descendants of Abraham. But under the new covenant, we are taught the gospel message first, and then we commit to the Lord Jesus. Unlike those under the old covenant those in the new covenant are taught first before they can be covenant related.

The new covenant says, *"They shall not teach everyone his fellow citizen, and everyone his brother, saying, 'Know the Lord,' for all will know Me, from the least to the greatest of them"* (Hebrews 8:11).

Fudge in commenting on this Scripture says:

BAPTISM WHAT IS IT GOOD FOR?

A second promise is that all who are God's people under the new covenant will know Him personally. **From the least to the greatest** no individual covered by the new arrangement is excluded. The covenant at Sinai was entered by a nation including many who did not know God personally until after they were involved in the covenant. All who were later born into the relationship as Jews had to be taught of God and learn of His former acts of deliverance and provision.

The new covenant is entered by individuals, one by one, and only on the knowledge of God and His saving acts in Christ (see John 6:44-45). Those entering the new covenant already know what God has done for them in the Son. They commit themselves to Him in confidence that His work is sufficient for their pardon and blessing. They signify both their knowledge and intention by the obedience of faith in baptism.

When one has entered this relationship with God as one among His covenant people, he already knows God as his own saving God. There is no need for those who are in the
covenant to be teaching each other a knowledge of God in this sense. Each **brother** and each **neighbor** or fellow-citizen in the new commonwealth already has that knowledge.[1]

Those in the New Covenant enter into that relationship with a basic knowledge of God, Jesus, sin, punishment, sacrifice, the new birth, commitment, and living a godly life, among other things. They must also learn about how they can get into a real relationship with God.

An important aspect of the New Covenant is that a person accepting Jesus as Lord and God is that they have heard enough information and evidence to commit. Jesus said, *"No one, after putting his hand to the plow and looking back, is fit for the kingdom of God"* (Luke 9:62b). Jesus is not looking for a casual disciple, but a committed one. Being a follower of Jesus requires discipleship. Discipleship implies self-denial, sacrifice, service, and even suffering.

CHAPTER THREE: THE OLD COVENANT VS THE NEW COVENANT

1. Edward Fudge, *Our Man in Heaven An Exposition of the Epistle to the Hebrews,* Baker Book House: Grand Rapids, Michigan, 1974, page 87.

CHAPTER FOUR:
JOHN THE BAPTIST'S BAPTISM WAS DURING THE OLD COVENANT

Who was John the Baptist? He and Jesus were physically related through their mothers. *"And behold, even your relative Elizabeth has also conceived a son in her old age; and she who was called barren is now in her sixth month"* (Luke 1:36). Gabriel said this to Mary when he announced that she would bear the Son of God. We don't know exactly what relation Elizabeth was to Mary. John was around six months older than Jesus.

The purpose of John was announced by an angel of the Lord to Zacharias, John's father. *"It is he who will go as a forerunner before Him in the spirit and power of Elijah, to turn the hearts of the fathers back to the children, and the disobedient to the attitude of the righteous, so as to make ready a people prepared for the Lord"* (Luke 1:17). John's purpose was to call people back to God and make them ready for Jesus.

John was preaching a call to repentance because the kingdom of heaven was at hand (Matthew 3:2). *"Then Jerusalem was going out to him, and all Judea and all the district around the Jordan; and they were being baptized by him in the Jordan River, as they confessed their sins"* (Matthew 3:5-6).

BAPTISM WHAT IS IT GOOD FOR?

"John the Baptist appeared in the wilderness preaching a baptism of repentance for the forgiveness of sins" (Mark 1:4).

"And he (John) came into all the district around the Jordan, preaching a baptism of repentance for the forgiveness of sins" (Luke 3:3).

When the Pharisees and Sadducees came out for baptism John, demanded proof of their repentant heart (Matthew 3:8).

"So he began saying to the crowds who were going out to be baptized by him, 'You brood of vipers, who warned you to flee from the wrath to come? Therefore bear fruit in keeping with repentance, and do not begin to say to yourselves, 'We have Abraham for our father,' for I say to you that from these stones God is able to raise up children to Abraham. Indeed the axe is already laid at the root of the trees; so every tree that does not bear good fruit is cut down and thrown into the fire" (Luke 3:7-9).

John's message was not only a call to get their hearts right by repenting in preparation for the coming of the Messiah, but a warning that wrath is coming. Matthew includes in his account, *"His winnowing fork is in His hand, and He will thoroughly clear His threshing floor; and He will gather His wheat into the barn, but he will burn up the chaff with unquenchable fire"* (Matthew 3:12).

Beasley-Murray says regarding Matthew 3:12:

> The Messiah is to use a winnowing fan, not however with the chief intent of gathering chaff for burning, any more than the farmer with whom the comparison is made is primarily concerned with dust; winnowing is for grain and grain is for the barn. The Messiah comes to gather the People of God and establish the Kingdom of God, and neither John nor his hearers could have thought otherwise.[1]

John's baptism was for repentance. He preached that they were to turn back to God, confess their sins, and believe in the one coming after him. When they were baptized, they received forgiveness of sins (Luke 3:3). *"As for me, I baptize you with water for repentance, but He who is coming after me is mightier than I, and I am not fit to remove His sandals; He will baptize you with the Holy Spirit and fire"* (Matthew 3:11).

John was the messenger, the preparer of the way for Jesus. *"The voice of one crying in the wilderness, make ready the way of the Lord, make His paths straight"* (Isaiah 40:3 quoted in Matthew 3:3, Mark 1:3, and Luke 3:4). The Gospel of John records John the Baptist telling those questioning him as to who he was since he was baptizing. He said that he was preparing the way for the Christ (John 1:19-28).

Beasley-Murray says:

> That the baptism administered by John awaits the Messiah's advent for its ratification in divine vindication, and the baptism administered in the

name of Jesus receives immediate response, is due to the distinction between the time of the Forerunner and that of the Risen Lord.[2]

John was instructing people to turn back to God and to look ahead to a coming Savior. Now we look back to the established Savior.

Refer to SPECIAL STUDIES: A1 THE NEW TESTAMENT HAS FIVE BAPTISMS for more on John's Baptism and its validity today.

CHAPTER FOUR: JOHN the BAPTIST'S BAPTISM DURING THE OLD COVENANT

1. G.R. Beasley-Murry, *Baptism in the New Testament*, William B. Eerdmans Publishing Company: Grand Rapids, Michigan, Reprinted March 1974, page 33
2. Ibid, page 103

CHAPTER FIVE:
JESUS IS BAPTIZED BY JOHN

The fact that Jesus was baptized should mean something to us. John said to Jesus, "You don't need to do this" (paraphrase). Jesus went through that baptism of repentance when He had nothing to repent of. The Scriptures make it clear that He was sinless. Yet, Jesus was baptized. Why did He consider it to be important? Jesus said to John, *"Permit it at this time; for in this way it is fitting for us to fulfill all righteousness"* (Matthew 3:15).

> *Then Jesus arrived from Galilee at the Jordan coming to John, to be baptized by him. But John tried to prevent Him, saying, 'I have need to be baptized by You, and do You come to me?' But Jesus answering said to him, "Permit it at this time; for in this way it is fitting for us to fulfill all righteousness.' Then he permitted Him. After being baptized, Jesus came up immediately from the water; and behold, the heavens were opened, and he saw the Spirit of God descending as a dove and lighting on Him, and behold a voice out of the heavens said, 'This is My beloved Son in whom I am well-pleased* (Matthew 3:13-17).

Two things happened after Jesus was baptized. The Spirit of God came upon Him, and the Father spoke His approval of His Son.

Jesus had no sin to repent of, so why be baptized? This has perplexed Christian scholars for centuries. Many reasons have been put forth. I have included a few that I believe will show us that even Jesus considered that baptism is necessary. Of course, in the case of Jesus's baptism it was John's baptism and not the baptism after the cross.

Consider Fowler's analysis:

> While forsaking sin and seeking forgiveness there from may be the first step in repentance toward God, a step not needed by the sinless Jesus, yet positive conformity to God's righteousness was most certainly required of Jesus. Thus, it becomes most intelligible and quite proper that Jesus should feel personally impelled to submit to John's immersion. He publicly declared thereby His resolve to surrender His will to the will of God, and His renunciation of all sin. He did this, not in spite of His Sonship, but on account of it! He knew that He was the pure Son of God, but this was good reason for obeying God: as a pure Son.[1]

Jesus submitted to the will of His Father in being baptized. It was only after His baptism that Jesus began His ministry. He performed signs, wonders, and miracles. He trained His successors and fulfilled His Father's will by being the sacrifice for all.

BAPTISM WHAT IS IT GOOD FOR?

Aylsworth says regarding the baptism of Jesus:

> Although Christ was baptized by John, his baptism differed in important respects from John's baptism; and in all these respects corresponded with Christian baptism, and with the advantage, that some of its attendant features are pictorially represented. It is an exact type of Christian baptism in all respects, save that the matter of sin does not enter into consideration. Let us notice what takes place here. First, we have the external act, which we can see; but we have also, on the part of Jesus, a putting off of the old, and laying on a new, life-work—a putting off of the life of a carpenter and taking up that marvelous mission of saving mankind. On the part of God, we have the performance of the physical baptism through John his appointed agent, and, in it, his approving acceptance of Jesus in his new consecration; for he openly declares such acceptance immediately after. Then, at the close of the act of baptism, the Spirit, in the form of a dove, appears and rests upon Jesus, and a voice out of heaven declares him to be God's well-beloved son.[2]

Aylsworth reminds us that Jesus had no sins when He was baptized. Therefore, Jesus' baptism did not involve repentance, only obedience to the Father's command.

Keep in mind that Jesus, after He was baptized, began a new life as a rabbi and not as a carpenter. When He came up out of the water, He received the Spirit and the Father's approval. What is implied by the words *"Fulfill all righteousness"* is that had He failed to do what the Father commanded; He would not have received the Father's approval.

There are major differences as well as parallels between Jesus's baptism and New Testament baptism as G.R. Beasley-Murry points out:

> Jesus was acknowledged Son of God at the Baptism (Mk. 1:11) and in Him we become sons of God in baptism by faith (Gal. 3:26f). The former citation is a proclamation of the messianic office of Jesus, the latter indicates the creation of a filial relationship to God. There is therefore a vast difference between the two experiences, yet there is also a connection between the two experiences.[3]

Jesus' baptism at around age thirty resulted in a Spirit-filled new life and a new career. Jesus clearly considered baptism to be essential to obedience and starting a new life, even for Himself.

R. C. Foster helps us to understand the importance of the statement Jesus made:

> It is extremely significant that the baptism of Jesus occurred at the very beginning of His ministry. As our baptism marks the dividing line between the old life of sin and the new life in Christ, so the baptism of Jesus is the dividing line between His

quiet life of seclusion at Nazareth and his public ministry. At the Jordan Jesus took the decisive step leaving behind Him home ties and setting forth with 'no place to lay His head" but with His great mission before Him.[4]

Jesus set an example for us in His being baptized. Foster continues:

> The baptism of Jesus is an important factor in the complete example He has given to us. "To fulfill all righteousness" is His motive. He humbled Himself to give us a complete example. It is not enough to know that the bread and wine symbolize His broken body and shed blood when we keep the Lord's Supper. Our hearts reach back to the upper chamber as well as Calvary and we delight to remember that He himself shared that first supper with the little group of Apostles. And so in His baptism He joined hands not merely with John, the multitudes, and God Himself, but also with all of us. When we come to obey our Lord in Christian baptism our hearts go back to the Mount of Ascension whence the Great Commission was given, but also to the Jordan where He gave the example. Is there a heart that does not quicken as he sees Jesus, the Son of God, humble Himself in the waters of the Jordan?[5]

When Jesus came forth from being immersed in the Jordan, the Spirit of God descended upon Him and God the

Father proclaimed, *"This is My beloved Son, in whom I am well pleased"* (Matthew 3:16-17).

Jesus rose up from being baptized and began a life that proclaimed God and was devoted to serving God officially.

Since Jesus submitted to baptism to fulfill all righteousness and He considered baptism a requirement even for Himself to please God, I have to ask, "Why would we not to submit to the Father's will regarding baptism following Jesus's example?"

We need to consider first what God has declared to be connected to our receiving salvation before we examine baptism. Remember John preached for the people to demonstrate their repentant heart before being baptized. It should be clear that for one to be ready to be baptized there must be a change of attitude and direction, a focus on God rather than on self. Therefore, we will start by examining what is connected with salvation.

CHAPTER FIVE: JESUS IS BAPTIZED BY JOHN

1. Harold Fowler, Bible Study Textbook Series, *The Gospel of Matthew,* Volume 1, College Press: Joplin, Missouri, 1981, page 116.
2. N. J. Aylsworth, *Moral and Spiritual Aspects of Baptism,* Christian Publishing Company: St. Louis, 1902, pages 63 & 64.
3. G.R. Beasley-Murry, *Baptism in the New Testament*, page 65.
4. R. C. Foster, *Studies in the Life of Christ,* Baker Book House: Grand Rapids, Michigan, 1975, pages 319 and 320.
5. Ibid, page 320.

CHAPTER SIX
SAVED BY FAITH: IS IT ENOUGH?

Grace is God's great gift of forgiveness offered on the basis of Jesus' sacrifice. Today many believe that grace means that you are saved by faith alone. What that means is that when you believe that Jesus died for you and accept that fact, you are immediately saved. Your sins are forgiven and you are born again through your belief and acceptance. All one has to do is believe in Jesus.

The most popular verse for those who believe we are saved by faith alone is John 3:16, *"For God so loved the world, that He gave His only begotten Son, that whoever believes in Him shall not perish, but have eternal life."* If we stop with this verse, then all we have to do is believe in Jesus. Within this verse there is no requirement to change our lifestyle or be baptized.

The writer of Hebrews says, *"And without faith it is impossible to please God, because anyone who comes to him must believe that he exists and that he rewards those who earnestly seek him"* (Hebrews 11:6 NIV).

However, if we read only Hebrews 11:6, we can say all I need to do is to believe in God and trust Him. Using this verse, I don't even have to acknowledge Jesus since He isn't mentioned in it.

The point is that if we build a case for salvation upon one verse and ignore other Scriptures, we will miss out. We must earnestly seek salvation and examine all the related Scriptures.

There are definite things that we must believe before we can proceed with God — first, that He exists, and second, that He keeps His promises. We must acknowledge that we are separated from God because of our personal sins, and for that reason, we need a Savior. We must believe that the only Savior is the only begotten Son of God, Christ Jesus (Acts 4:12). Yes, we must have faith! If faith is all that is required of us, is there any real call for commitment? How about obedience? If only my faith saves me, then the implication is that I am home free without doing anything else.

Jesus gave an illustration in John 15:1-8. He said that He is the true vine and those in Him are the branches. The branches are required to bear fruit which they can do only because they are attached to the vine. Jesus said, *"If anyone does not remain in me, he is like a branch that is thrown away and withers; such branches are picked up, thrown into the fire and burned"* (John 15:6 NIV). When we are united with Christ Jesus, He requires and expects us to bear fruit. If we aren't bearing fruit, then we are cast away from Him.

You may ask, "But we are saved by faith. Is not faith by itself enough because our works don't save us?

James wrote, *"You believe that God is one. You do well; the demons also believe, and shudder. But are you willing to recognize, you foolish fellow, that faith without works is useless?"* (James 2:19-20). James uses Abraham's example of offering Isaac as a sacrifice and Rahab's helping the spies (James 2:21-25). *"You see that a man is justified by works and not by faith alone"* (James 2:24). According to James for faith, to be real, it must be demonstrated by actions. James Chapter Two teaches that faith alone is not of any real value.

Joseph B. Mayor writes:

> But in the midst of this diatribe against a dead faith, St. James gives some further particulars of a true faith, such as Abraham's (ver. 22): faith cooperated with his works and by works was faith made perfect; words which are in close agreement with St. Paul's teaching as to faith 'which worketh by love,' and the 'fruits of the Spirit.[1]

Many have rejected what James has written because it seems to stand against what Paul wrote concerning works. However, Paul is dealing with works and law keeping as a way of earning salvation. Paul's conclusion is that no one can do anything in order to earn salvation. James is dealing with work as proof that your faith is real and not as a way to earn salvation. It is important to understand that while we cannot do anything to earn salvation, God still expects obedience and demonstration of our faith by what we do with our life. Do not forget that *"God demonstrated His own love"* (Romans 5:8a). When you read the word of God, look at all the times that God demonstrated faithfulness, power, love, justice, and mercy. Therefore, why should we expect to escape from needing to demonstrate our faith by what we do?

William Barclay commented on Paul and James's writings says:

> (i) We begin by noting that James's emphasis is in fact a universal New Testament emphasis. It was the preaching of John the Baptist that men should prove the reality of their repentance by the excellence of their deeds (*Matthew* 3:8; *Luke* 3:8). It was Jesus's preaching that men should so live that the world might see their good works and give the glory to God (*Matthew* 5:16) .... Nor is this emphasis missing from Paul himself. Apart from anything else, there can be few teachers who have ever stressed the ethical effect of Christianity as Paul does. However doctrinal and theological his letters may be, they never fail to end with a section in which the expression of Christianity in deeds is insisted upon.[2]

Many have used Galatians 2:16 as a basis for proving that we are justified by faith alone. *"We are Jews by nature and not sinners from among the Gentiles; nevertheless knowing that a man is not justified by works of the Law but through faith in Christ Jesus, even we have believed in Christ Jesus, so that we may be justified by faith in Christ and not by the works of the Law; since by the works of the Law no flesh will be justified"* (Galatians 2:15-16).

Consider, *"Now that no one is justified by the Law before God is evident; for, THE RIGHTEOUS MAN SHALL LIVE BY FAITH"* (Galatians 3:11). Paul uses Habakkuk 2:4 to make the point quoting, *"THE RIGHTEOUS MAN SHALL LIVE BY HIS FAITH."*

Merrill C. Tenney says this about the word *Law* in Galatians, "The meaning of the term is quite clearly defined in Galatians 3:17, where the law is identified with the Mosaic code of spiritual, moral, and ceremonial principles."[3]

If we are going to be saved by Law keeping, we have to be as perfect as God Himself. *"For whoever keeps the whole law and yet stumbles at just one point is guilty of breaking all of it"* (James 2:10 NIV). If a man breaks one piece of the law, he must pay the penalty. A law keeper has to be one-hundred percent perfect; even ninety-nine-point ninety-nine percent does not count. Fail to keep one piece of the law, and one-hundred percent goes down to zero percent. We need to understand that law presents rules which must be obeyed and penalties for breaking the rules. Law makes no provision for grace, but only punishment for disobedience.

In the Galatians letter, one thing that Paul is dealing with is the Judaizing teachers who were trying to bind physical circumcision upon Gentile converts to Christ. The answer of the Spirit through Paul is, *"And I testify again to every man who receives circumcision, that he is under obligation to keep the whole Law. You have been severed from Christ, you who are seeking to be justified by law; you have fallen from grace"* (Galatians 5:3-4). If you try to be justified by meritorious works, earning your justification, then you have rejected God's great gift of grace. Simply said, you cannot be saved by works and grace. *"I do not nullify the grace of God, for if righteousness comes through the Law, then Christ died needlessly"* (Galatians 2:21). If I determine to earn my salvation or even try to pay for part of salvation by my good works, then I reject Christ's atoning death as meaningless.

The difference between James and Paul is what they are addressing regarding justification. Paul clearly states that you cannot be justified by keeping law or by working for justification, whereas James says that your actions demonstrate that you have faith. Paul, you cannot earn salvation; James, your works demonstrate that your faith is real. Both are in complete agreement.

Joseph B. Mayor in commenting on the idea of Paul versus James says:

> The two main points at issue are (1) the necessity of works, (2) Abraham's justification by faith. James had said over and over again 'Faith without works is dead' (ii 17, 20, 24, 26); his meaning being (as is plain from ver. 14, and the illustration of a philanthropy which is limited to words (vv. 15, 16), as well as from the whole tone and argument of the Epistle), not to depreciate faith, which is with him not less than with St. Paul the very foundation

of the Christian life. (cf. i. 3, 6, ii. 1, v. 15), but to insist that faith, like love, is valueless, if it has no effect on the life, but expends itself in words.[4]

Barclay says, "The fact that Christianity must be ethically demonstrated is an essential part of the Christian faith throughout the New Testament."[5]

Faith by itself that does not lead to a changed life is worthless. Know that a person's faith in God must be seen through his actions. Justification is the free gift from God based on Jesus' sacrifice, and that can only be accepted, not earned. After the great discourse on grace in Ephesians Chapter Two Paul writes, *"For we are God's workmanship, created in Christ Jesus to do good works, which God prepared in advance for us to do"* (Ephesians 2:10 NIV).

"For by grace you have been saved through faith; and that not of yourselves, it is the gift of God; not as a result of works, so that no one may boast" (Ephesians 2:8-9). We are saved by grace and not works thanks to God's loving mercy. Yet James says that works are necessary to prove our faith to be genuine. The works that we do after being a Christian do not contribute to our salvation. Those works can accomplish Jesus' tasks handed down to His people with His power working through His followers.

What exactly is involved in salvation? Is there more than faith? Moses led a people out of Egyptian slavery. God promised them a land, a rich land. They had to have faith in, or to put it another way, trust God to keep His promise.

BAPTISM WHAT IS IT GOOD FOR?

They witnessed His awesome power in the plagues, crossing the Red Sea, and in His providing them with water and manna. They were not allowed into the promise land, or as the Hebrew writer says, God's rest (Hebrews 3:7-11,16-17). *"And to whom did He swear that they would not enter His rest, but to those who were disobedient? So we see that they were not able to enter because of unbelief"* (Hebrews 3:18-19). The people led out of Egypt did not get to the Promised Land because of their lack of faith and disobedience. God later rejected the first king of Israel, Saul because of his disobedience (I Samuel 15:22-23).

There are two things coupled with receiving what God has promised. Those two things are belief and obedience. The generation led out of Egypt by Moses lost out on what God promised by their lack of belief and obedience. Samuel confronted Saul for disobeying God's commandment to destroy the Amalekites totally (I Samuel 15:18). Saul spared the king and blamed the people for saving forbidden items (I Samuel 15:3, 20-21). *"Samuel said, 'Has the Lord as much delight in burnt offerings and sacrifices as in obeying the voice of the Lord? Behold, to obey is better than sacrifice, and to heed than the fat of rams. For rebellion is as the sin of divination, and insubordination is as iniquity and idolatry, because you have rejected the word of the Lord, He has also rejected you from being king"* (I Samuel 15:22-23).

Note that disobedience is rebellion against God's authority. Therefore, obedience is necessary to avoid displeasing God. What do we do with Jesus, who has been given all authority in both heaven and earth, and who has ordered us to go and baptize (Matthew 28:18-20)?

We must understand that obedient faith is required. Therefore, action on our part is necessary to lay hold of God's saving grace. Faith alone is not sufficient; it is but the beginning step.

Someone gives you a million-dollar home. All the taxes and fees are paid, and it is completely free with no strings attached. It is free for you to move in and enjoy. You have done nothing to deserve or to earn that gift. The gift is there waiting. The giver is standing there with the deed and keys in his hand waiting. But you say, "It is a free gift. I don't have to do anything; it is mine." The giver looks at you and holds out the deed and the keys waiting. Understand that as with any free gift, there is a needed response on the receiver's part. He has to accept the gift before he can enjoy it. We all accept the fact that we have an action we must do to claim any free gift. We have to reach out and take the deed and keys to possess that free gift.

Is belief the only requirement, or is it the foundation? You can read John 3:16 as a stand-alone verse and see that belief is all that is required. However, there are many other verses that talk about eternal life and salvation or redemption that add more than belief.

Eternal life or salvation is a free gift (Romans 6:23). There is nothing I can do to earn salvation, as a song says, "Jesus paid it all." My salvation is 100% free, but there are conditions that must be fulfilled. To accept the free grace of God I must do so by obedient faith. Remember what Jesus said after His resurrection, *"All authority in heaven and on earth has been given to me"* (Matthew 28:18 NIV). Jesus has been declared by the Father King of kings and Lord of lords. I cannot disregard my Lord's commandments or set them aside. Therefore, I cannot be saved on believing only without a definite response on my part.

Faith in Jesus Gives Us The Right to Act upon That Belief And Become A Child of God

If we look at faith as the only necessary thing on our part to receive salvation, we need to consider John 1:12 which says, *"But as many as received Him, to them He gave the right to become the children of God, even to those who believe in His name."*

> Vine tells us that the word in the original language which the NASB among others translates as *right* is *exousia:* "A. Noun ... authority, power, is translated "right" in the RV, for KJV, "power" in John 1:12" ... Exousia first denotes "freedom to act" and then "authority for the action."[6]

Our faith in Christ Jesus according to John 1:12 gives us the right to become children of God. We can act upon our faith and become a child of God, or we can fail to act. Belief in the name of Jesus empowers us to act upon our faith. Some action on our part coupled with our belief in Christ Jesus enables us to become children of God.

"Yet to all who received him, to those who believed in his name, he gave the right to become children of God" (John 1:12 NIV).

Frank Pack comments on *the right*, "Men are given the **power** (exousia) or "right" (ASV, NEB) to become God's children. To have this right men must receive Christ, they must believe **in his name.**"[7]

John clearly says that we are not made children by believing, but Jesus gives the believer who receives Him the power to become the child of God. Therefore, it seems that simple belief by itself does not make one God's child.

James Burton Coffman writes:

> **Gave them the right ...** The privilege of being a child of God is the greatest privilege afforded by life on earth; but even when people have complied with the conditions antecedent to the gift, no one can ever be considered as deserving or meriting so marvelous a gift. The disagreements of people regarding the terms of salvation should never obscure the truth that salvation **CANNOT** be earned or merited by mortal man. Conditions there certainly are, else salvation would have to be universal; but when all conditions are complied with, the sinner is still saved by grace.[8]

Unless we have a firm belief in Jesus as deity, His atoning sacrifice, and His resurrection, becoming a child of God is impossible. If belief in Jesus was all that God requires, then even the demons would have the right to be saved.

Faith in The Power of Jesus' Sacrifice

> *But God demonstrates His own love toward us, in that while we were yet sinners, Christ died for us. Much more then, having now been justified by His blood, we shall be saved from the wrath of God through Him. For if while we were enemies we were reconciled to God through the death of His Son, much more having been reconciled, we shall be saved by His life (Romans 5:8-10).*

When we say that we need to do something in addition to Christ Jesus' sacrifice we are denying that His death paid for our sins. There is absolutely nothing we can do that earns us any part of salvation. Jesus has done everything needed to redeem us from God's wrath.

Around seven hundred years before Jesus' crucifixion, God spoke through Isaiah:

> *Surely our griefs He Himself bore, and our sorrows He carried; yet we ourselves considered Him stricken. Smitten of God and afflicted. But He was pierced through for our transgressions, He was crushed for our iniquities; the chastening for our well-being fell upon Him, and by His scouring we are healed. All of us like sheep have gone astray. Each of us has turned to his own way, but the Lord*

has caused the iniquity of us all to fall on Him (Isaiah 53:4-6).

Jesus took our punishment upon Himself. He was tried and convicted without real evidence, beaten severely, mocked, publicly humiliated, and executed in a most barbaric manner. This was done to Him by mankind, the very mankind that He created. If that were not bad enough, the Father dumped all our sins, past, present, and future on Him. He had every sin since Adam and Eve of every single human being who has ever lived or will ever live put on Him. Then the Father turned away from His Son, and Jesus was symbolically cast into the outer darkness away from His Father. He cried out, *"My God, My God why have You forsaken Me?"* (Matthew 27:46c) He who was with God in the beginning and was God (John 1:1-2) was symbolically separated from the Father not because He sinned, but because He had our sins placed upon Himself.

To help us better understand Jesus' sacrifice, we must look at the Day of Atonement under the Law of Moses (Leviticus 16:1-34). The Day of Atonement was once a year. The high priest first had to offer a bull for his sins and for his household. The high priest could not enter the Holy of Holies until he offered the bull. Then he took the two goats already chosen and presented them before the Lord. He cast lots for the two goats. One was to be a sacrifice for the Lord, the other became a scapegoat. One goat was slaughtered and its blood was taken into to Holy of Holies as the sacrifice for the sins of the people. After atonement was made, the high priest went to the scapegoat, laid both hands on the goat's head, and confessed all the sins of the people, putting their sins on the goat's head. The goat was led out by a man into the desert where it was released. Thus, their sins were taken away. Under the Law of Moses there was a blood sacrifice to pay the price for sin. Then there was a visual removing sin far away with the scapegoat. David wrote, *"As far as the east is from the west, so far He has removed our transgressions from us"* (Psalm 103:12).

In the book of Hebrews, we read that God has declared Jesus to be the High Priest (Hebrews 5:1-10). Unlike the high priests before Him, Jesus did not have to offer a sacrifice for His own sins because He had none. Speaking of Jesus Christ, who is righteous, John wrote; *"And He Himself is the propitiation for our sins; and not for ours only, but also for those of the whole world"* (I John 2:2). Propitiation is a hard word for many; basically, it conveys the idea of satisfaction. By the sacrificial shedding of His blood Jesus became the means by which our sins are paid for in full. Consider that Jesus was taken out of the city and crucified. *"Therefore Jesus also, that He might sanctify the people through His own blood, suffered outside the gate"* (Hebrews 13:12). Jesus had the sins of mankind placed upon Him. Like the scapegoat He carried our sins away. When we are in Christ Jesus our sins are gone. God no longer remembers our sins (Hebrews 8:12). The apostle Paul wrote; *"God made him who had no sin to be sin for us, so that in him we might become the righteousness of God"* (II Corinthians 5:21). The Son of God serves as High Priest, blood sacrifice, and scapegoat to redeem us.

In order for that to happen Jesus had to undergo a horrible death. Knowing what was coming it is no wonder the night Jesus was betrayed He prayed three times to the Father and asked for another way (Matthew 26:36-44). *"In the days of His flesh, He offered up both prayers and supplications with loud crying and tears to the One able to save Him from death, and He was heard because of His piety"* (Hebrews 5:7).

"Although He was a Son, He learned obedience from the things which He suffered, and having been made perfect, He became to all who obey Him the source of eternal salvation" (Hebrews 5:8-9).

Jesus was obedient to the Father's will and carried out God's plan of redemption. Note that the Hebrew writer does not say, *"to all who believe in Him"*, but *"to all who obey Him."* Along with faith at the bottom line is obedience. To paraphrase James, "Faith without obedience is worthless."

Understand while obedience is required, obedience without faith is worthless. Faith or trust in Jesus and what He has done to redeem us is an absolute bottom-line requirement.

When we believe in Jesus, what are we led to do? We will follow His example of belief in God and obedience to Him.

On the day of Pentecost when the gospel message was preached, we read that the Jews who heard the message that Jesus was both *"Lord and Christ"* (Acts 2:36b), responded. *"Now when they heard this, they were pierced to the heart, and said to Peter and the rest of the apostles. "Brethren, what shall we do?"* (Acts 2:37). Learning of their sins and that Jesus died, was buried, and rose, they believed in Jesus. They wanted to know what they could do because they now believed and were convicted of their sin of rejecting God's anointed One.

"Peter said to them, 'Repent. And each of you be baptized in the name of Jesus Christ'" (Acts 2:38a). After they were convicted concerning Jesus, the first thing they were told to do was repent. Repentance was coupled with baptism. However, before we touch on repentance, we need to understand the basis for faith.

CHAPTER SIX: SAVED BY FAITH

1. Joseph B. Mayor, *The Epistle of St. James The Greek Text with Introduction and Comments,* Second Edition, Baker Book House: Grand Rapids, Michigan, 1978 from the 1897 edition, page 210.
2. William Barclay, *the Letters of James and Peter,* Revised Edition, The Daily Bible Study Series, The Westminster Press: Philadelphia, 1976, page 72.
3. Merrill C. Tenney, *Galatians: The Charter of Christian Liberty,* Revised and Enlarged Edition, WM. B. Eerdmans Publishing Co.: Grand Rapids, Michigan, 1975. Page 156.
4. Joseph B. Mayor, page xci.
5. Barclay, page 73.
6. *Vine's Expository Dictionary of Biblical words,* page 534.
7. Frank Pack, *The Gospel According to John*, Part I 1:1-10:42, Frank Pack, Sweet Publishing Company: Austin, Texas, 1975, page 34.
8. James Burton Coffman, *"Commentary on John".* "Coffman Commentaries on the Old and New Testament". https://www.studylight.org/commentaries/bcc/john-1.html. Abilene Christian University Press: Abilene, Texas, USA. 1983-1999.

CHAPTER SEVEN
HEARING THE GOSPEL: THE BASIS FOR FAITH

How do we acquire faith in Jesus and God? We are told that, *"Without faith it is impossible to please Him"* (Hebrews 11:6a). We read, *"So faith comes from hearing, and hearing by the word of Christ"* (Romans 10:17). Faith is based on knowledge which is acquired by hearing Christ's word. We must learn about God and Jesus before we gain faith. Christian faith is not blind, but faith is based solidly upon furnished information and witnessed facts.

Hendriksen says:

> What Paul is saying, then, is that faith in Christ presupposes having heard the word that proceeds from and concerns Christ ... The great importance Paul attached to *hearing* immediately reminds one of Jesus. In all Christ's teaching, both on earth and from heaven, it would be difficult to discover any exhortation which he repeated more often, in one form or another, than the one about hearing; better still: listening.[1]

We can come to the conclusion by observing the universe and nature that there has to be a Creator behind this very complex and well-functioning universe.

> *Since what may be known about God is plain to them, because God has made it plain to them. For since the creation of the world God's invisible*

> *qualities — his eternal power and divine nature — have been clearly seen, being understood from what has been made, so that men are without excuse (*Romans 1:19-20 NIV).

Lee Strobel, in his book *The Case for a Creator,* cites Werner von Braun, the father of space science.

> *The vast mysteries of the universe should only confirm our belief in the certainty of its Creator. I find it as difficult to understand a scientist who does not acknowledge the presence of a superior rationality behind the existence of the universe as it is to comprehend a theologian who would deny the advances of science.*[2]

As we examine the universe, the only conclusion that we can arrive at is that there is design to it. As complex as it is, it cannot have just happened on its own. Therefore, there has to be a rational intelligent mind behind the universe.

Brad Harrub writes, "A God that can create the world can surely communicate His Will to His creation."[3]

It can be understood that God who is love, righteous, just, and jealous for His people; who is light, in whom there is no darkness; and who is wrathful must by His very nature communicate with His creation. Not only that, He will protect His word throughout the centuries. If He doesn't, then He has forfeited His right to hold us accountable for what we have done with the life He has blessed us with. It is not the point of this book to prove that God is. There are many excellent books on the existence of God and on the faithfulness of the Scriptures if one needs to examine the evidence.

Jesus said, *"Heaven and earth will pass away, but my words will never pass away"* (Matthew 24:35 NIV). Isaiah wrote, *"The grass withers and the flowers fall, but the words of our God stands forever"* (Isaiah 40:8 NIV).

The only way that we really learn about the true and living God is through the book that is called the Bible.

Henry H. Halley said:

> We believe the Bible to be, not man's account of his effort to find God, but rather an account of God's effort to reveal Himself to man: God's own record of His dealings with men, in His unfolding revelation of Himself to the human race: the Revealed Will of the Creator of Man, given to Man by the Creator Himself, for the Instruction and Guidance in the Ways of Life.[4]

All Scripture is God-breathed and is useful for teaching, rebuking, correcting and training in righteousness, so that the man of God may be thoroughly equipped for every good work" (II Timothy 3:16-17 NIV). *"His divine power has given us everything we need for life and godliness through our knowledge of him who called us by his own glory and goodness* (II Peter 1:3 NIV).

Remember Hebrews 8:11, *"They shall not teach everyone his fellow citizen, and everyone his brother, saying, 'Know the Lord,' for all will know Me, from the least to the greatest of them."* A person entering into a relationship with God learns of God and Jesus before being in that relationship. The previous covenant that God made with the Israelites that He brought out of Egypt was one in which a male child was circumcised at eight days, and he was then in covenant with God. However, he then had to learn who God was and what his responsibly toward the covenant was. In the Christian Era we learn of God, what He has done, and what is expected of us so that we can choose to commit, understanding the cost.

"Now which I make known to you, brethren, the gospel which I preached to you, which also you received, in which also you stand, by which also you are saved" (I Corinthians 15:1-2a).

- Paul had preached the gospel to the Corinthians.
- The Corinthians had received the gospel.
- They stood in the gospel.
- They were saved by the gospel.

Just what is the gospel? Paul goes on in I Corinthians 15 to tell us what the gospel is. *"For I delivered to you as of first importance what I also received, that Christ died for our sins according to the Scriptures, and that He was buried, and that He was raised on the third day according to the Scriptures"* (I Corinthians 15:3-4). The gospel is simply that Jesus Christ died because we sinned, He was buried, and He was raised. All this was prophesied in the Old Testament. The gospel preached was:

- Christ died for our sins.
- He was buried.
- He stayed in the tomb for three days.
- He was raised on the third day.

Paul goes to list in verses 5-9 the multitude of eye witnesses to Jesus's resurrection who were still living more than twenty years after the resurrection (I Corinthians 15:5-9). Paul wrote I Corinthians around 55 A.D., there were more than 514 actual witnesses to Jesus' resurrection, most of whom were alive then. This is important historical information. The resurrection did not happen out in the desert; it happened in Jerusalem. The Jewish leaders could not deny that the tomb was empty. There were too many eye witnesses to Jesus' death and to the fact that the tomb was empty.

For some people, this is all they need to hear. Others need to learn that the Scriptures came from God and that they are completely reliable or that Jesus is real.

Basically, we need to know our need for a Savior because of our selfish and sinful life. We need to believe Jesus is our Savior because He took God's wrath upon Himself and shed His blood paying the price that we owed for our sins. His resurrection is the proof that He is the Savior. *"But God raised him from the dead, freeing him from the agony of death, because it was impossible for death to keep its hold on him"* (Acts 2:24 NIV). Because Jesus was resurrected, we know that He is Lord and Christ or Messiah (Acts 2:36).

Therefore, the Gospel is the basis of our faith. Knowledge of the Gospel is the firm foundation needed so that we can understand what God has done for us.

CHAPTER SEVEN: HEARING THE GOSPEL: THE BASIS FOR FAITH

1. William Hendriksen, *Exposition of Paul's Epistle to the Romans,* New Testament Commentary, Baker Academic: Grand Rapids, Michigan, 2007, page 351.
2. Lee Strobel, *The Case for a Creator,* Zondervan, Willow: 2004, page 273.
3. Brad Harrub, *Convicted A Scientist Examines the Evidence for Christianity,* Focus Press, Inc: 2011, page 99.
4. Henry H. Halley, *Halley's Bible Handbook,* Zondervan Publishing House, Grand Rapids, Michigan: 1963, page 22.

CHAPTER EIGHT:
SAVED BY REPENTANCE

To repent involves change. In the case of a sinner who is seeking God, he repents because of God-centered sorrow over his sin. A worldly person has sorrow over the fact of being caught. "For the sorrow that is according to the will of God produces a repentance without regret, leading to salvation, but sorrow of the world produces death" (II Corinthians 7:10).

James Burton Coffman says, "Repentance is not sorrow for sin, which in many cases is mere "sorrow of the world" due to the inconvenience caused by sin or its discovery."[1]

A person who is sorry for having sinned doesn't necessarily purpose not to repeat that sin again. Just because he got caught with his hand in the cookie jar doesn't mean that he won't try again. Being sorry for being caught only makes one more careful when committing that sin again.

Coffman continues, "Even godly sorrow is not repentance, but a condition that produces repentance."[2]

Say to them, "As I live!' declares the Lord God, 'I take no pleasure in the death of the wicked, but rather that the wicked turn from his way and live. Turn back, turn back from your evil ways! Why then will you die, O house of Israel? (Ezekiel 33:11).

BAPTISM WHAT IS IT GOOD FOR?

Repentance is turning from a life that is self-directed to a God-directed life. It indicates a desire for a new purpose to life and a sorrow for the past life.

F. LaGard Smith has this to say about repentance:

> In the process of repenting, we take measure of our lives and admit that we are lacking. Repentance is a time of spiritual reflection that calls us to be painfully honest and to see the need to straighten out our lives — the need to make the rough ways smooth. Repentance is the willingness to let Christ fill our emptiness and lead us in new directions. Without this compliant attitude, we will never enjoy God's salvation.[3]

Jesus, in commenting on Galileans who were killed by Pilate when they were offering sacrifices, said that they didn't die because they were any worse sinners than any other Galileans. Jesus said, *"I tell you, no, but unless you repent, you will all likewise perish"* (Luke 13:1-3).

H. Leo Boles wrote this about Luke 13:1-3:

> In answer to the question Jesus raised, he said of them that no such preeminence in sin is to be attributed to them. It is wrong to conclude that their fate was due to any great wickedness that they had committed. "Except ye repent, ye shall all in the like manner perish." This declaration brings their attention to their own sin ... "Repent" is used many times in the New Testament. It means a change of

mind, disposition, governing purpose; unless one changes from an impenitent heart doom, certainly awaits one. The suffering of these becomes a warning to all others to repent or to perish. There is no alternative; it is either repent or perish[4]

William Hendriksen says:

Jesus is simply telling the people that unless they experience a complete and radial change they *also* will perish. Not for a moment should they imagine that they can escape the judgement of God just because they happen to be the seed of Abraham.[5]

Jesus clearly offers a choice — repent or perish. Jesus calls us from a self-directed life to a God-directed life. *"I know, O Lord, that a man's way is not in himself, nor is it in a man who walks to direct his steps"* (Jeremiah 10:23). We need direction in our lives. Left to our own choices, we choose sin.

We might ask, "Doesn't grace cover all that?" When we believe, aren't we covered by grace? If I believe and ask Jesus into my heart, I must be okay with God. If I have to repent to avoid perishing, that's a work on my part and grace is a free gift of God. Therefore, since I am saved by grace, repentance is not necessary.

"Therefore repent and return, so that your sins may be wiped away, in order that times of refreshing may come from the presence of the Lord" (Acts 3:19). But that was

said by Peter to the Jews who had rejected Jesus. Therefore, does that apply to us? Paul said:

> *So, King Agrippa, I did not prove disobedient to the heavenly vision, but kept declaring both to those of Damascus first, and also at Jerusalem and then throughout all the region of Judea, and even to the Gentiles, that they should repent and turn to God, performing deeds appropriate to repentance* (Acts 26:19-20).

Paul states that Gentiles also must repent and turn to God. Included in that statement is that deeds which clearly demonstrate true repentance must be evident.

Note that the Jews, who were covenant related to God and rejected Jesus, were told to **return** to God. Whereas the Gentiles, who had not been covenant related to God, were told to **turn** to God.

Two things are demanded of Jew and Gentile — repent and turn to God's leadership over your life. Why? "So that your sins may be wiped away." Let us couple this statement with gaining eternal life just by believing. If all you have to do is believe and you have eternal life without repentance, it then follows that you still have your sins. According to Acts 3:19, your sins are not wiped away until you repent and come back to God.

Consider the following thoughts. McGuiggan states concerning sin:

> Once a sinner, always a sinner! From the moment of my first sin, I can never be as though I have never sinned, from that moment on, my blessed state before God as someone forgiven is different from the blessedness of the sinless ones.
>
> The person whose sin is not imputed (counted against, EJW) to him or her is a very different being from the person who never committed sin. It was not sin that sinned — I sinned and changed my state before God.
>
> But the good news begins with the word "repent." Because it is an imperative — "Repent!" — it isn't an option. There is no negotiation. But because it is an imperative, it tells us we aren't beyond redemption; by his grace, we are *able* to turn to him! God would not call a corpse to repent; he would not call to repentance what is incapable of repenting.[6]

The great thing about our heavenly Father is that He desires us to be with Him throughout eternity and not separated from Him. Therefore, He has made provision for us to be able to come to or to return to Him. After we believe in God, we need to honestly acknowledge that we are sinners and make the decision to turn from a sinful, self-directed life to a life in submission to our Father.

BAPTISM WHAT IS IT GOOD FOR?

McGuiggan goes on to say about this:

> However precisely we would define the relation of repentance to forgiveness, this we know: *without repentance, there is no forgiveness!*
>
> Repentance looks back in sorrow at where we've been and forward with eagerness to a holy life that knows full forgiveness. Repentance is a mind that by God's grace renounces the sinful past as unacceptable and purposes a future pleasing to God.[7]

We must understand that without sincere sorrow over our sins, asking forgiveness from our Father, and an attitude that like God in which there is a hatred of sin, not sinners, we will not please our Father.

Of John the Baptist it is said, *"And he came into all the district around the Jordan, preaching a baptism of repentance for the forgiveness of sins"* (Luke 3:3). Peter said, *"Therefore repent and return, so that your sins may be wiped away, in order that times of refreshing may come from the presence of the Lord"* (Acts 3:19). Repentance is connected with the forgiveness of sins or having your sins wiped away.

Smith says, *"This penitent attitude and willingness to be transformed is at the core of our baptism. It prepares the way for the salvation to come."*[8]

We also must consider the attitude in true repentance. *"Blessed are those who mourn, for they shall be comforted"* (Matthew 5:4). *"For the sorrow that is according to the will of God produces a repentance without regret, leading to salvation, but the sorrow of the world produces death"* (II Corinthians 7:10).

Spiros Zodhiates comments on Matthew 5:4:

> The sorrow that is sanctified by the Saviour's benediction exists in the heart — often as a principle, occasionally as a passion, which mourns and grieves because of sin as a thing hateful in itself, rather than because the consequences of that sin are injurious to his comfort and peace.[9]

John, in writing to believers says, *"If we confess our sins, He is faithful and righteous to forgive us our sins and to cleanse us from all unrighteousness"* (I John 1:8). While this is directed to believers, the principle applies to those coming to Christ Jesus. Our Father does not need to be told that we have sinned; He knows it. We are the ones who must own up to our sins. If we try to consider them as mistakes, minor things, or simply excuse them, then our Father cannot forgive them or accept our repentance. Like our Father, we must be honest and we must hate sin.

Zodhiates continues, "The sorrow that the blessed person feels extends not only to the sins that are known, or public, but to secret sins."[10]

BAPTISM WHAT IS IT GOOD FOR?

David said, *"Who can discern his errors? Acquit me of hidden faults"* (Psalm 19:12). Job said, *"If I have done iniquity, I will not do it again?"* (Job 34:32). While Job believed that he was suffering for no reason, certainly not because he sinned, his attitude should be our attitude.

When a person repents, he must make a personal acknowledgement of sin and an acceptance of personal responsibility in committing sin. No excuses like, "The devil made me do it," or "I'm only human." There must be sorrow for having sinned against God and a realization that sin is hateful to God. Then comes confession of sin seeking pardon and the hatred of sin as well. Thus, the commitment to turn from sinning comes about.

Thus far we see that several things are tied into having our sins forgiven. First, *"For by grace you have been saved through faith; and not of yourselves, it is the gift of God"* (Ephesians 2:8). Second is believing in God's Son, *"Whoever believes in Him shall not perish, but have eternal life"* (John 3:16). Third is repentance for the forgiveness of sins (Acts 3:19 and 26:19-20). Fourth is a change of direction to go God's way (Acts 3:19 and Acts 26:19-20).

God's part is granting grace while our part consists of faith, repentance, and turning to God, but is there anything else in God's word tied to salvation, eternal life, and forgiveness of sins?

CHAPTER EIGHT: SAVED BY REPENTANCE

1. James Burton Coffman, *Commentary on 1 and 2 Corinthians,* Firm Foundation Publishing House, Box 610, Austin, Texas 78767, 1976 page 400.
2. Ibid, page 400.
3. F. LaGard Smith, *Baptism: The Believer's Wedding Ceremony,* Cotswold Publishing, 2013, page 37.
4. H. Leo Boles, *New Testament Commentaries Luke,* Gospel Advocate Company, Nashville, Tenn,, 1977, page 268.
5. William Hendriksen, *New Testament Commentary, Exposition of the Gospel According to Luke,* Baker Academic, Grand Rapids, Michigan, 1978, page 694.
6. Jim McGuiggan, *The God of the Towel,* Howard Publishing Co., West Monroe, Louisiana, 1997, pages 91-92.
7. Ibid, page 92.
8. F LaGard Smith, page 36.
9. Spiros Zodhiates, *The Pursuit of Happiness,* AMG Press, Chattanooga, TN., 1981, page 240.
10. Ibid, page 240.

CHAPTER NINE:
SAVED BY CONFESSING JESUS AS LORD

The righteousness based on faith and not law keeping is being discussed by Paul in Romans 10. *"But what does it say? 'The word is near you, in your mouth and in your heart'—that is, the word of faith which we are preaching, that if you confess with your mouth Jesus as Lord, and believe in your heart that God raised Him from the dead, you will be saved"* (Romans 10:8-9). If you confess that Jesus is Lord verbally and believe that God raised Him from the dead, ***"You will be saved".***

Beasley-Murry says:

> Here it is evident that faith is directed to the Lord for the purpose or with the result of receiving righteousness, and confession is made in order to receive, or with the effect of receiving salvation; the point of the bestowal of the gift is not mentioned, but it is not needful to do so…[1]

So, simply believing that God raised Jesus from the dead and saying out loud that Jesus is Lord saves you? However, if we just go by Romans 10:8-9, there is no apparent need to repent and turn to God. All that is necessary is believing that God raised Jesus from the dead and verbally confessing your faith. In the previous chapter we saw that repentance is absolutely required by God. Therefore, it is logical to understand that confessing your belief by itself is not enough to save anyone.

Jesus said concerning confession, *"Therefore everyone who confesses Me before men, I will also confess him before My Father who is in heaven"* (Matthew 10:32). This is addressed to His followers. Christians must not be silent or ashamed to confess their belief in Jesus as Lord, God, and Savior.

William Hendriksen, in talking about Matthew 10:32, says:

> To profess — or "confess" — Christ means to acknowledge him as Lord of one's life, and to do so openly ("before men"), even in the hearing of those who were opposing him.[2]

Jesus said, *"But whoever denies Me before men, I will also deny him before My Father who is in heaven"* (Matthew 10:33). Keeping silent is not an option, even in the face of death.

"Whoever confesses that Jesus is the Son of God, God abides in him, and he in God" (I John 4:15). The confession is our acknowledgement that Jesus is truly the Son of God. When Jesus asked His disciples who He is, Peter answered Him. *"You are the Christ, the Son of the living God"* (Matthew 16:16).

BAPTISM WHAT IS IT GOOD FOR?

Salvation, forgiveness of sins, and eternal life are gained by:

- Grace which comes freely from God.
- Faith, belief in God's Son which is action by a person.
- Repentance, sorrow for sins also an action performed by a person.
- Turning to God's direction or leadership is an action done by a person.
- A person's confession that Jesus is the Son of God.

God's grace, faith, repentance, surrendering to God's will, and confession also result in salvation, but where does baptism fit in? So, can we pick and choose? Or are all these things involved in bringing us to the point of salvation?

Consider carefully my next point. If Christ had never died on the cross, there would be no way a righteous and just God could forgive anyone without violating His nature. God's grace is based on Christ's obedient death on the cross. Christ offered Himself freely in our place. He redeemed us by paying the debt that we owe. Once we have heard and believe that Jesus died for us, we should have great sorrow which leads to repentance for our sins that put Him on the cross. We then turn away from our self-directed lives to a God-directed life and confess Jesus as our redeemer. Up to this point, I believe the majority of believers will say, "Amen!"

Paul wrote to Timothy:

> *Fight the good fight of the faith. Take hold of the eternal life to which you were called and about which you made the good confession in the presence of many witnesses. I charge you in the presence of God, who gives life to all things, and of Christ Jesus, who in his testimony before Pontius Pilate made the good confession, to keep the commandment unstained and free from reproach until the appearing of our Lord Jesus Christ* (I Timothy 6:12-14 ESV).

Faithful public confession of Jesus as "My Lord and my God" is required from believers throughout their lives.

F.F. Bruce says regarding confession, "In apostolic times it is plain that baptism followed immediately upon confession of faith in Christ."[3]

CHAPTER NINE: SAVED BY CONFESSING AS LORD

1. G. R. Beasley-Murray, page 103.
2. William Hendriksen, *New Testament Commentary Exposition of the Gospel According to Matthew,* Baker Academic, Grand Rapids, Michigan, 2007, page 473.
3. F. F. Bruce, *The Epistle of Paul to the Romans,* page 136.

CHAPTER TEN
SAVED BY BAPTISM

When God's patience waited in the days of Noah, while the ark was being prepared, in which a few, that is, eight persons, were brought safely through water. Baptism, which corresponds to this, now saves you, not as a removal of dirt from the body but as an appeal to God for a good conscience, through the resurrection of Jesus Christ (I Peter 3:20b-21 ESV).

Peter plainly says that baptism saves us.

Noah and his family were saved by being in the ark from God's wrath. If Noah and his family had not built the ark according to God's specifications and gotten into it, they too would have perished in the Flood. The ark is used as an example of what baptism does. Just as the ark saved them from God's wrath baptism saves us from God's wrath.

"Whoever believes and is baptized will be saved, but whoever does not believe will be condemned" (Mark 16:16, ESV).

Mark connects baptism clearly with salvation. By coupling belief and baptism Mark says that without faith, baptism is worthless. I have been told by some who reject baptism that since Mark does not include baptism with not believing, baptism is not connected with salvation. I say that without believing in God nothing can save me. I cannot do enough good, I cannot be a good enough person, and I cannot devise a ritual that will save me. As Mark points out, unbelief condemns me.

As to the argument that because only not believing is connected with condemnation in Mark 16:16 negating baptism as necessary to salvation, baptism without belief does nothing but gets one wet. Belief is the basis of faith on which we come to God. Without belief salvation is impossible; therefore, it is irrelevant to include baptism as a condition of condemnation.

There are those who say baptism is done after being saved, either as a next step in commitment or membership in the church. The problem with this view is by putting baptism after salvation, many scriptural aspects of baptism are negated. Romans Six and Colossians Two, for example, teach baptism puts us unto unity with Jesus' death and our body of sin is done away with in baptism. Acts 2:38 equates baptism with forgiveness of sins and receiving the Holy Spirit. Baptism puts one in Christ, and outside of Him there is no salvation. Therefore, belief that baptism is done after being saved is not a valid belief.

Arndt and Gingrich say the meaning of the Greek word for *saves* in 1 Peter 3:21 is *"Of qualities, etc., that lead to salvation."* And of the same Greek word used for *saved* in Mark 16:16, they say, *"Pass. Be saved, attain salvation."*[1] Pass. Stands for passive voice, meaning that something is done to the person. In I Peter 3:21 the person is saved.

Baptism is a passive act on the part of the one being immersed. It is a submission to the will of God, an acceptance of Jesus as Lord and a point of commitment to serve Him. Remember that even Jesus submitted to being baptized. John knew that Jesus had no sins, and therefore, no reason to repent. John consented when Jesus said that it is to fulfill all righteousness. After Jesus was baptized, the Spirit of God came upon Him. The Father said that He loved His Son and was well pleased with His action (Matthew 3:13-17). Baptism is passive, whereas hearing, believing, repenting, and confessing are active in nature.

Consider also the book of Acts written by Luke.

Peter ended his sermon in Acts Chapter Two with, *"Therefore let all Israel be assured of this; God has made this Jesus, whom you crucified, both Lord and Christ. When the people heard this, they were cut to the heart and said to Peter and the other apostles, "Brothers, what shall we do?"* (Acts 2:36-37 NIV). Listen carefully to the reply. *"Repent and be baptized, every one of you, in the name of Jesus Christ for the forgiveness of your sins, and you will receive the gift of the Holy Spirit"* (Acts 2:38 NIV).

Note that they were told to repent and be baptized. This was in order that their sins could be forgiven and that they would be gifted with the Holy Spirit.

In relating his own baptism, Paul said that Ananias told him, *"Get up and be baptized, and wash away your sins, calling on His name"* (Acts 22:16b).

In these two accounts we learn our sins are removed during baptism.

BAPTISM WHAT IS IT GOOD FOR?

Carefully think on these verses that talk about the result of being baptized:

> *Or do you not know that all of us who have been baptized into Christ Jesus have been baptized into His death? Therefore we have been buried with Him through baptism into death, so that as Christ was raised from the dead through the glory of the Father, so we too might walk in newness of life. For if we have become united with Him in the likeness of His death, certainly we shall also be in the likeness of His resurrection, knowing this that our old self was crucified with Him, in order that our body of sin might be done away with, so that we would no longer be slaves to sin; for he who has died is freed from sin* (Romans 6:3-7).

Regarding Acts 2:38, some argue that the word *for* can be translated *because of*. Therefore, baptism is done because sins have been forgiven. There are problems with that. Let's look at several verses:

- Acts 2:38 would then read repent and be baptized because your sins have been forgiven. If your sins are already forgiven why repent after the fact. Since repentance and being baptized are connected with the word *and* they cannot be separated. The sentence would need to read, "Repent for the forgiveness of your sins and be baptized because your sins are forgiven."

- Acts 22:16b Paul understood that he still had his sins when he was told by Ananias, *"Get up and be baptized, and wash away your sins, calling on His name."*
- Romans 6:3-7, says that we are buried with Jesus through baptism and then raised to a new life, a life now freed from sin.

Therefore, baptism precedes forgiveness of sins.

The following chapters will examine baptism in greater detail so that we can gain a sound scriptural understanding of it. Baptism has been considered by many as a work done by the one being baptized. However, since salvation is by grace, there is no work that will earn man salvation. *"For by grace you have been saved through faith. And this is not your own doing; it is the gift of God, not a result of works, so that no one may boast"* (Ephesians 2:8-9 ESV). In Chapter Twelve it is shown that baptism is a work. However, while baptism is a work, it is a work done by God and not man.

In the next chapter we will examine Matthew 28:18-28 which contain Jesus' final instructions to His followers.

CHAPTER TEN
SAVED BY BAPTISM

1. William F. Arndt and F. Wilbur Gingrich, *A Greek-English Lexicon of the New Testament and Other Early Christian Literature,* The University of Chicago Press, licensed to Zondervan Publishing House. Fourteenth Impression 1973, page 806.

CHAPTER ELEVEN
AN EXAMINATION OF MATTHEW 28:18-20

Let us now look at New Testament baptism beginning with a critical look at these verses which are known as "The Great Commission," or the marching orders given to Christ's church.

"And Jesus came up and spoke to them, saying, "All authority has been given to Me in heaven and on earth, Go therefore and make disciples of all the nations, baptizing them in the name of the Father and the Son and the Holy Spirit, teaching them to observe all that I commanded you" (Matthew 28:18-20).

These are Christ Jesus' final orders to His followers. This command is a key to understanding the need for baptism. An important fact to note in Jesus' words in these verses is that the baptism is to be done by those He commanded. He did not say, "Make disciples and I will baptize them."

Jesus spent three years teaching His disciples by word and example. He commands His followers to teach others, and they are then to teach others and so on until the Lord returns. Matthew 28-18-20 is a clear command to Jesus' followers to evangelize.

1. Jesus makes the claim for having all authority in heaven and on earth. God the Father has given Jesus the Son total authority. Refer to Philippians 2:9-10 and Ephesians 1:22-23.

BAPTISM WHAT IS IT GOOD FOR?

2. Jesus demands His followers extend this invitation to everyone when He says *"all nations."*
3. Jesus says to make disciples. A disciple is a student or pupil. Jesus' followers are told to make students and followers of Him.

Boles writes:

> To disciple a person to Christ is to lead that one to become a follower of Christ, to be a learner in his school, to be obedient to his commands, to become a Christian. To 'make disciples' means to give all kinds of instruction for entrance into the church of our Lord.[1]

4. Baptism is administered by Christ's followers under the authority of the Trinity or Godhead which consists of Father, Son, and Holy Spirit. Baptism is a submissive and obedient act on the part of the believer being baptized. As such, it is not a work on the part of the disciple. Rather, it is an act of surrender to the will of Christ.
5. Note that to be a candidate for baptism, one has to be discipled or taught first. Boles says, "Those who are 'discipled' are to be baptized; they were not to baptize 'all the nations,' but those of 'all nations' who were 'discipled.'"[2]
6. I realize that many define "disciple" as a committed follower, i.e., one who is saved, but I am looking at "disciple" as simply a student. I base my premise on Hebrews 8:11 which says, *"No longer will a man teach*

his neighbor, or a man his brother, saying. 'Know the Lord,' because they will all know me, from the least of them to the greatest" (NIV). People must be taught about Jesus and the Gospel and know what is required of them before they commit to being a Christian. Without an understanding of who Jesus is and understanding that a commitment to Him as Lord over one's life is required, baptism is valueless.

7. After one is baptized, he needs to be taught all that Jesus taught the apostles. This is required for all Christians. It is a lifetime of learning, living and working for Jesus, and maturing in the faith.

To sum up, Jesus has total authority and commands Christians to make disciples of everyone who responds to being taught the Gospel and to baptize them by God's authority and then continue their education.

Consider baptism as the formal point of commitment and submission to Jesus as your personal Lord and God. Baptism is a bowing of your knee, accepting Jesus as Lord of your life, and of accepting Jesus as your Savior.

CHAPTER ELEVEN: AN EXAMINATION OF MATTHEW 28:18-20

1. H. Leo Boles, *A Commentary on The Gospel According to Matthew,* Gospel Advocate Company: Nashville, Tenn. 1976, page 564.
2. Ibid, page 564.

CHAPTER TWELVE:
JESUS AND GOD'S WORK IN OUR BAPTISM

Many have declared baptism to be a work. They have indicated that it is a work of man, and since we are saved by grace, baptism cannot be connected to salvation. However, the Scriptures make the point that baptism is a submissive act on the part of man. In baptism God is preforming work on man and baptism is but one work that God preforms on us that leads to our salvation.

What God does first is to draw us to Jesus. Jesus said, *"No one can come to Me unless the Father who sent Me draws him, and I will raise him up on the last day"* (John 6:44).

We have within us an emptiness needing to be filled. There are many things that will partially satisfy that emptiness. Work, family, pleasure, addictions, and anything else may dull that emptiness. Somewhere in our journey through life we hear about God and Jesus, and we are drawn to learn more. The emptiness can only be truly filled by a relationship with our Creator.

Butler says about God's part is drawing us to Jesus.

> God draws men to Jesus by the death of Jesus on the cross. ... No man can come to Jesus as Savior and King in the full sense until God has by His divine plan provided the mysterious drawing power of the cross. ... The drawing is to be done by hearing 'from the Father,' i.e., hearing the Word of God and learning the Way of Life.[1]

BAPTISM WHAT IS IT GOOD FOR?

In speaking of His manner of death, Jesus said, *"And I, if I am lifted up from the earth, will draw all men to Myself"* (John 6:32). His sacrificial death given freely for us has a drawing power to it.

Pack says, "**Draw** shows that Christ has power to attract man to himself through his death on the cross. Through Christ God draws all men (6:44)."[2]

The apostle Paul comments on the cross, *"For indeed the Jews ask for signs and Greeks search for wisdom; but we preach Christ crucified, to Jews a stumbling block and to Gentiles foolishness, but to those who are the called, both Jews and Greeks, Christ the power of God and the wisdom of God"* (I Corinthians 1:23-24).

God calls us through the gospel message to Christ. The gospel message shows us what Christ Jesus did for us. Paul wrote in I Corinthians 15:3-4 that the gospel or good news is that "Christ died for our sins," and "He was buried" and "He was raised on the third day." All this can be found in the word of God. Hebrews 11:6 says that God will reward those who seek Him.

Paul makes it abundantly clear by writing, *"For by grace you have been saved through faith; and that not of yourselves, it is the gift of God; not as a result of works, so that no one may boast"* (Ephesians 2:8-9). I can only through the faith which God has provided obtain what I needed to know so that I could have faith enough to accept His free gift of salvation. Jesus accomplished my salvation upon the cross totally. Knowing the gospel, I was drawn to Jesus as Savior and God.

Consider what Paul wrote concerning Christ:

> *For in Him all the fullness of Deity dwells in bodily form, and in Him you have been made complete, and He is the head over all rule and authority; and in Him you were also circumcised with a circumcision made without hands, in the removal of the body of the flesh by the circumcision of Christ; having been buried with Him in baptism, in which you were raised up with Him through faith in the working of God, who raised Him from the dead* (Colossians 2:9-12).

The following points are made in Colossians 2:9-12:

- Jesus is God, and He was God in the flesh while He walked among us.
- When we are in Christ Jesus, we are complete.
- We are reminded that Jesus is totally in charge.
- In Jesus we are circumcised, which is the removal of the body of flesh. The circumcision is done by Christ, not by men.
- We are buried with Him in baptism.
- We were then raised up through faith in God's power or God's working.
- The proof of our resurrection is that God raised His Son from the dead.

Circumcision Is A Work of Jesus That Is Done to Us.

In the Old Testament starting with Abraham, circumcision was a physical sign that a male belonged to God. Under the Law it was a sign that males were covenant related to God from the time they were eight days old. Now in Colossians 2:11 we read that we are circumcised by Christ. So, what is the difference? One major difference is that physical circumcision was for males only, whereas the circumcision made without hands is for male and female.

Wilbur Fields says about circumcision, "Circumcision was an essential act to be in covenant relationship with God, but the act was rendered worthless if the person's life was ungodly."[3] Circumcision is meaningless if the person is not committed to living a godly life.

The concept of circumcision seems to be abrupt in verse Colossians 2:11, but it is also mentioned in verse 13, *"When you were dead in your transgressions and the uncircumcision of your flesh, He made you alive together with Him, having forgiven us all our transgressions."* Prior to baptism we were dead and uncircumcised. Then when we were raised, we were made alive and circumcised.

A.S. Peake writes:

> The Apostle does not merely leave them with the statement that they have been made full in Christ, which rendered circumcision unnecessary, but adds that they have already

received circumcision, not material but spiritually, not the removal of a fragment of the body, but the complete putting off of the body of flesh.[4]

Circumcision for the Christian is connected with a putting off or shedding of the body of flesh. Clearly, we are not talking about our spirit discarding the physical body. Turning to Marshall for a translation of the Greek in verse 11, we read, "In whom also ye were circumcised with a circumcision not handwrought by the putting off of the body of the flesh, by the circumcision — of Christ"[5]

Christ gives us the perfect circumcision which is accomplished in baptism. That circumcision of removal of the flesh is an act by God. We are talking about Jesus cutting our ties with our old nature centered around our desires and wants. The center of our universe is no longer ourselves, but Christ. It is a change of heart and of mind. We must desire Christ so much that we allow Him to change us, or better said, we submit to Jesus.

Beasley-Murray says on putting off of the flesh, "It should not go unnoticed that the ending of an old existence (putting off the old man) and the beginning of a new one in Christ is the same reality as that represented under the image of dying and rising with Christ."[6]

In Christ we are given a clean life. The old selfish, lustful, and sin-stained life has been cut away by Christ. As in baptism as pictured in Romans 6 when Jesus circumcised us, our old nature is sacrificed so that we now have a Christ-centered life which controls us rather than our wants and desires. It is one thing to struggle with our old nature and another to say, "Great. I am under grace now," and continue living the same as before.

God Unites Us with Jesus' Death Where Sin Is Done Away with and We Die to Sin.

"Having been buried with Him in baptism" (Colossians 2:12a). *"Or do you not know that all of us who have been baptized into Christ Jesus have been baptized into His death"* (Romans 6:3). In the act of baptism, we are united with Jesus' death.

When we are buried with Christ in baptism, we are separated from being governed by fleshly desires.

Following a discussion on grace in Romans Chapter Five, Chapter Six begins, *"What shall we say then? Are we to continue in sin so that grace may increase? May it never be! How shall we who died to sin still live in it?"* (Romans 6:1-2).

Just how did we die to sin? Did I die to sin by deciding to refuse to sin anymore on my own? Does God have a part in my dying to sin?

To find out how we die to sin read on in Romans 6. *"Or do you not know that all of us who have been baptized into Christ Jesus have been baptized into His death?"* (Romans 6:3).

Everyone who has been baptized, without exception, was baptized into Christ Jesus. Baptism unites us with Christ.

In fact, baptism joins us to His sacrificial death on the cross.

> *Therefore we have been buried with Him through baptism into death, so that as Christ was raised from the dead through the glory of the Father; so we too might walk in newness of life. For if we have become united with Him in the likeness of His death, certainly we shall also be in the likeness of His resurrection, knowing this, that our old self was crucified with Him, in order that our body of sin might be done away with, so that we would no longer be slaves to sin; for he who died is freed from sin* (Romans 6:4-7).

- Baptism buries us with Jesus where we join with His death. We are joined with His atoning sacrifice. Another way to put it is that by submitting to being baptized we have decided to die to our selfish nature.
- Just as Christ was raised by the Father's glory, we are raised.
- We are united with Jesus' death in which He shed His blood and took our justly earned punishment upon Himself. Jesus paid our penalty. *"The blood of Jesus His Son cleanses us from all sin"* (I John 1:7c).
- Knowing that He was raised, we know that we will be raised just like He was.
- Our old self was nailed to the cross as He was nailed to the cross. When He died, Jesus circumcised everyone who comes to Him. That

circumcision cuts away the body of flesh, doing away with our old nature of slavery to sin. (Colossians 2:11)
- We now have a new life.
- We have a new righteous life when we are in Christ. *"He (God) made Him (Jesus) who knew no sin to be sin on our behalf, so that we might become the righteousness of God in Him"* (II Corinthians 5:21).

Jesus Makes Us Righteous When We Are United with Him.

Our faith does not make us righteous. Our good deeds do not make us righteous. Our obedience does not make us righteous. Performing a ritual does not make us righteous. Jesus makes us righteous when we are in Him. *"For all of you who were baptized into Christ have clothed yourselves with Christ"* (Galatians 3:27, NIV).

Hendriksen writes, "All those, then, who by means of their baptism have truly laid aside, their garment of sin, and have truly been decked with the robe of Christ's righteousness, having been buried with him and raised with him, have put on Christ."[7]

Strong references, "William Ashmore holds that incorporation into Christ is the root idea of baptism, union with Christ's death and resurrection being only a part of it. We are "baptized into Christ" (Rom. 6:3), as the Israelites were "baptized into Moses" (I Cor. 10:2)."[8]

Being united with Christ Jesus is essential as it is the only way that God is able to accept us. *"Salvation is found in no one else, for there is no other name under heaven given to men by which we must be saved"* (Acts 4:12 NIV).

Jesus Himself said the night that He was betrayed, *"No one comes to the Father except through me"* (John 14:6b NIV). There simply isn't another way to God. We must come to God through Jesus. Jesus through His sacrifice reveals God's redemptive grace and unites us with the Father. In Him and Him alone are we righteous, and that is due through grace and no works of our own.

"Or do you not know that the unrighteous will not inherit the kingdom of God" (I Corinthians 6:9)? Paul in his discussion regarding the non-Jews and Jews says, *"What then? Are we better than they? Not at all: for we have already charged that both Jews and Greeks are all under sin: as it is written, THERE IS NONE RIGHTEOUS, NOT EVEN ONE"* (Romans 3:9-10). All humanity is equal because all are sinners.

Therefore, if we are not clothed in Jesus, we have no hope. Only by being in Him can we enter God's presence. The penalty for any and all sin is eternal separation from God. There is no lesser penalty. Only the fact that Jesus took our place and our punishment after He had led a totally sinless life grants salvation.

It is important to know that there are two basic things that God requires and they are faith and obedience. God makes us righteous, as though we have never sinned, when we are clothed in His only begotten Son. Baptism is the only way to be clothed in Jesus.

God Gives Us A Brand New and Clean, Godly Life.

"We were therefore buried with him through baptism into death in order that, just as Christ was raised from the dead through the glory of the Father, we too may live a new life" (Romans 6:4 NIV).

Dave Miller writes:

> When the penitent (repentant [EJW]) believer allows himself to be lowered into the watery grave of baptism. That is **the moment** he contacts the blood of Christ which was shed in Christ's death. Hence, Romans 6:3-4 explains that when we are baptized in water, we are baptized **into Christ's death** — the contact point for forgiveness. Being "buried with Him through baptism into death" is the point at which we are cleansed of sin, thus enabling us to "walk in newness of life." According to the sequence stipulated in the passage, we cannot have "newness of life" until **after** we come up out of the waters of baptism.[9]

When we have the new life in Christ, we are freed from our old life. However, it involves a changed mindset. Consider what Paul wrote in Colossians Chapter Three.

> *Keep seeking the things above ... not the things that are on earth ... consider the members of your earthly body as dead to ungodly behavior ... in them you also once walked ... put them all aside ... have put on the new self who is being renewed to a true knowledge according to the image of the One who created him* (Colossians 3:1-10).

In coming to Christ Jesus, we agree to God's condemnation of the sin in which we walked. Like God, we now hate sin. We have determined to strive to resist living by the flesh or sin. In other words, we have decided to die to sin when we come to be united with Jesus. *"Therefore do not let sin reign in your mortal body so that you obey its lusts, and do not go on presenting the members of your body to sin as instruments of unrighteousness; but present yourselves to God as those alive from the dead, and your members as instruments of righteousness to God"* (Romans 6:12-13).

In Christ we now have God's help in resisting temptation. *"No temptation has overtaken you but such as is common to man; and God is faithful, who will not allow you to be tempted beyond what you are able, but with the temptation will provide the way of escape also, so that you will be able to endure it"* (I Corinthians 10:13).

In Hebrews Chapter Ten the Spirit through the author is contrasting the priesthood under the Law with the priesthood of Jesus. *"And since we have a great priest over the house of God, let us draw near with a sincere heart in*

BAPTISM WHAT IS IT GOOD FOR?

full assurance of faith, having our hearts sprinkled clean from an evil conscience and our bodies washed with pure water" (Hebrews 10:22).

The one who wrote Hebrews reminds us that when the Old Law was inaugurated, the book, the people, the tabernacle, and all the vessels used in worship were sprinkled with blood (Hebrews 9:18-21). *"Indeed, under the law almost everything is purified with blood, and without the shedding of blood there is no forgiveness of sins"* (Hebrews 9:22, ESV).

The people and everything used for worship were sprinkled with blood and made pure and set apart to God. Likewise, Christians are purified and set apart to God by the sprinkling of their hearts by the blood of Christ. This cleansing that was done was necessary to make us a fit place for being the temple of the Holy Spirit. *"Or do you not know that your body is a temple of the Holy Spirit within you, whom you have from God? You are not your own, for you have been bought with a price. So glorify God in your body"* (I Corinthians 6:19-20, ESV).

Because of Jesus, our great priest, we can draw near to the throne of God. As the Lamb, Jesus was the sacrifice whose blood is greater than that of bulls and goats. His blood had to be offered only once for all time. As high priest, Jesus presented the sacrifice before God in heaven.

Therefore, we have complete confidence in the grace of our great priest that He has cleansed our hearts so that our evil conscience no longer stands in the way of approaching the holy God. Our hearts have been sprinkled with the blood of Christ Jesus.

We read in Titus, *"He saved us, not on the basis of deeds which we have done in righteousness, but according to His mercy, by the washing of regeneration and renewing by the Holy Spirit"* (Titus 3:5). The bottom line is that our salvation rests solely on God's mercy and grace. We are being renewed into the image that we were created in, and even that is a work of God through the Spirit.

"But we all, with unveiled face, beholding as in a mirror the glory of the Lord, are being transformed into the same image from glory to glory, just as from the Lord, the Spirit" (II Corinthians 3:18).

"Our bodies washed with pure water" (Hebrews 10:22d).

R. Milligan quoted Alford: "Indeed nearly all eminent expositors are now agreed that there is here a manifest reference to the ordinance of Christian baptism. Alford says, 'There can be no reasonable doubt that this clause refers directly to Christian baptism'"[10]

Peter used the ark in which eight people came safely through the flood as a type of baptism. He even linking baptism with our conscience.

"Corresponding to that, baptism now saves you—not the removal of dirt from the flesh, but an appeal to God for a good conscience—through the resurrection of Jesus Christ" (I Peter 3:21).

BAPTISM WHAT IS IT GOOD FOR?

Baptism now saves us. Not by washing the physical dirt off of our bodies, but an appeal is made to God through baptism for a good conscience. This gets back to obedient faith on our part.

Consider what William Barclay says about I Peter 3:18-22.

> Peter has been speaking about the wicked men who were disobedient and corrupt in the days of Noah; they were ultimately destroyed. But in the destruction by the flood eight people — Noah and his wife. His sons Shem, Ham, and Japheth, and their wives — were brought to safety in the ark. Immediately the idea being brought to safety through the water turns Peter's thoughts to Christian baptism, which is also a bringing to safety through the water. What Peter literally says is that baptism is an antitype of Noah and his people in the ark.[13]

By their obeying God and being in the ark Noah and his family were saved from the cleansing of evil from the world by water. Now in a similar way, our obedience to Jesus by being baptized removes the influence of sin. *"We know that our old self was crucified with him in order that the body of sin might be brought to nothing, so that we would no longer be enslaved to sin"* (Romans 6:6, ESV).

Barclay goes on to give three great things about baptism from these verses:

> (i) Baptism is not merely a physical cleansing: it is a spiritual cleansing of the whole heart and soul and life. Its effect must be on a man's very soul and on his whole life.
>
> (ii) Peter calls baptism the pledge of a good conscience to God (verse 21). The word Peter uses for pledge is *eperōtēma*. In every business contract there was a definite question and answer which made the contract binding. The question was, "Do you accept the terms of this contract, and bind yourself to observe them?" And the answer before witnesses was: "Yes." Without that question and answer the contract was not valid.... Peter is in effect, saying that in baptism God said to the man coming direct from heathenism, "Do you accept the terms of my service? Do you accept its privileges and promises, and do you undertake its responsibilities and its demands?" And in the act of being baptized the man answered: "Yes."
>
> (iii) The whole idea and effectiveness of baptism is dependent on the resurrection of Jesus Christ. It is the grace of the Risen Lord which cleanses us; it is to the Risen, Living Lord that we pledge ourselves; it is to the Risen, Living Lord that we look for strength to keep the pledge that we have given.[12]

BAPTISM WHAT IS IT GOOD FOR?

Noah demonstrated his faith and obedience to God by building the ark exactly to God's requirements, putting everything God commanded into the ark, and getting into the ark with his family. Thus, Noah and his family were brought safely through the water.

The Spirit speaking through Peter tells us that baptism is a demonstration of our faith and obedience by using Noah and the ark as an example. When we are baptized, we accept the Lord Jesus Christ as Ruler of our lives. We confess with our mouths that Jesus is Lord, and we demonstrate our commitment by being baptized.

Many have denied baptism because they have considered it a work on the part of the one being baptized. Of course, we accept that salvation is based on grace and not our workings. However, when baptism is understood as a submission on the part of the believer, things change. Yes, baptism is a work. But not a work of man; it is God's work. God begins the work of transforming the submissive believer into the image of Christ when he is born again.

We can sum up what God does to us in the submissive act of baptism. God works to first draw us to Jesus Christ. He unites us with the sacrificial death of His Son. He washes away our sins in the blood and cleanses our conscience. He circumcises us, separating us from our sinful nature. He raises us up to a new life. God also promises help in resisting temptation so that we will not fall back into a life of sin.

CHAPTER TWELVE: JESUS AND GOD'S PART IN BAPTISM

1. Paul T. Butler, *Bible Study Textbook The Gospel Of John, Vol, I,* College Press, Joplin, Missouri, 1981, page 246.
2. Frank Pack, *The Living Word Commentary* Editor Everett Ferguson, *The Gospel According to John Part II, 11:1-21:25,* Sweet Publishing Company, Austin, Texas, 1977, pages 34-35.
3. Wilbur Fields, *Philippians-Colossians Philemon, Bible Study Textbook Series,* College Press, Joplin, Missouri, 1969, page 183.
4. A.S. Peake, *The Epistle To The Colossians, V, The Expositor's Greek Testament, Volume Three,* Edited by W, Robertson Nicoll, WM. B. Eerdmans Publishing Company, Grand Rapids, Michigan, 1974, page 524.
5. Alfred Marshall, *The Interlinear Greek-English New Testament,* Regency Reference Library, Zondervan Publishing House, Grand Rapids, Michigan, 1958, page 794.
6. Beasley-Murray, Page 149.
7. William Hendriksen, *New Testament Commentary Exposition of Galatians, Ephesians, Philippians, Colossians, and Philemon,* Baker Academics, Grand Rapids, Michigan, 2007, page 149.
8. Augustus Hopkins Strong, *Systematic Theology,* Three Volumes in One, Fleming H. Revell Company, Old Tappan. New Jersey, 1976. Page 941.

9. Dave Miller, *Baptism & the Greek Made Simple,* Apologetics Press, 210 Landmark Drive, Montgomery, Al 36117. 2019, page 78.
10. R. Milligan, *New Testament Commentary Vol.IX.— Epistle To The Hebrews,* Gospel Advocate Co., Nashville, Tenn., 1954, page 282.
11. William Barclay, *The Daily Study Bible Series, the Letters of James and Peter Revised Edition,* 1976, page 243.
12. Ibid, pages 244, 245.

CHAPTER THIRTEEN
WHY DO WE NEED JESUS?

This is a valid question. After all, there are plenty of "good" people in the world who are not Christians. Surely God will not cast them away.

From the time God evicted Adam and Eve from the garden until the covenant that God made with the Israelites through Moses, mankind lived under the Patriarchal Age. The Patriarchal Age was when the father was the main ruler when it came to religion. Job is an example. He offered up sacrifices for his family (Job 1:5). During this time God also had priests. Melchizedek, *"A priest of God Most High"* was an example (Genesis 14:18c). Even before the Covenant made on Mount Sinai, God required blood to cover sins. Since Adam all mankind had been looking forward to the perfect sacrifice offered one time for all time.

God made a covenant with the Israelites, whom He brought out of slavery at Mount Sinai through Moses (Exodus 19-24). At that time, they were to be God's special people. Solomon prayed at the dedication of the Temple,

> *Also concerning the foreigner who is not of Your people Israel, when he comes from a far country for Your name's sake (for they will hear of Your great name and Your mighty hand, and of Your outstretched arm); when he comes and prays*

BAPTISM WHAT IS IT GOOD FOR?

> *toward this house, hear in heaven Your dwelling place, and do according to all for which the foreigner calls to You, in order that all the peoples of the earth may know Your name, to fear You, as do Your people Israel, and that they may know this house which I have built is called by Your name* (I Kings 8:41-43).

The Israelites were to set an example in faithfulness and show God to all who passed through Israel. They also had instructions for converting Gentiles. God has always had provision for those who seek Him to find Him. In the Book of Jonah, we find that God sent Jonah to Nineveh to warn them of eminent destruction for their sins. Jonah preached God's message, the people of Nineveh repented, and God spared them. God has always desired and wanted a restored relationship with all mankind.

God made provision for covering the penalty under the old covenant. That provision was animal sacrifices. However, animal sacrifices were not the final solution. *"For it is impossible for the blood of bulls and goats to take away sins"* (Hebrews 10:4). Those animal sacrifices could never work because an animal is not equal to a human. The sacrifice had to be a human who was himself free from sin. Only then could that person be an acceptable sacrifice for sinful humanity. That sacrifice was Jesus. *"For this reason He is the mediator of a new covenant, so that, since a death has taken place for the redemption of the transgressions that were committed under the first covenant, those who have been called may receive the promise of the eternal inheritance"* (Hebrews 9:15). Jesus' blood reaches back to creation.

Have this mind among yourselves, which is yours in Christ Jesus, who, though he was in the form of God, did not count equality with God a thing to be grasped, but emptied himself, by taking the form of a servant, being born in the likeness of men. And being found in human form, he humbled himself by becoming obedient to the point of death, even death on a cross" (Philippians 2:5-8 ESV). God the Son stepped down from the throne, laid down His rights and privileges, and submitted to entering the physical universe as a Jewish baby who was born into a working-class family. Jesus the Christ grew up obedient to God the Father and God's plan of redemption of being the perfect sacrifice so that our sins can be wiped out. Because of His obedience and the Father's declaration, Jesus is our High Priest. *"For we do not have a high priest who is unable to sympathize with our weaknesses, but one who in every respect has been tempted as we are, yet without sin"* (Hebrews 4:15, ESV).

It is amazing the Son of God gave up the throne and His rights and privileges of Deity. Jesus kept His divine nature and yet was capable of being tempted. He was still God; that is undisputed. There is no sin in God, and that is undisputable. God also cannot be tempted, *"For God cannot be tempted by evil"* (James 1:13c, NIV). God by His nature with no evil in Him cannot be tempted, so how can the Son of God, God in the flesh be really tempted like you and me? Yet, in order to be the perfect high priest and the perfect sacrifice, Jesus had to able to be disobedient, and He had to be capable of committing sin.

Our comfort is that we know Jesus felt the full power of temptation as all mankind does. Because He knew that His Father was God, I believe that He was empowered to resist. If we remember that in Christ, we are a child of God, and we have the power to resist temptation. Knowing our relationship with the heavenly Father, we have the power to resist temptation if we avail ourselves of that the power.

We understand that Jesus kept the old covenant perfectly. He did not break one law or rule. Hence, He is able to take our penalty upon Himself since He was sinless. Paul said of what God did, *"He made Him who knew no sin to be sin on our behalf, so that we might become the righteousness of God in Him"* (II Corinthians 5:21). This was God's plan even before creation. Note that the only way we can be righteous is by being in Jesus.

Consider what God directed Isaiah to write around 700 years prior to His sending Jesus:

"But He was pierced through for our transgressions, He was crushed for our iniquities; the chastening for our well-being fell upon Him. And by His scourging we are healed" (Isaiah 53:5). Jesus stepped up and took upon Himself our justly earned punishment. Only God's love for humanity could cause Him to offer His only begotten Son, and obedience and love could cause God's Son to take our punishment upon Himself.

F. Delitzsch says:

> The meaning is not that it was our sins and iniquities that had pierced Him through like swords, and crushed Him like heavy burdens, but that He was pierced and crushed on account of our sins and iniquities. It was not His own sins and iniquities, but ours, which He had taken upon Himself, that He might make atonement for them in our stead, that were the cause of His having to suffer so cruel and painful a death.[1]

In carrying out the Father's plan of redemption, Jesus willingly accepted all the sins of all mankind from Adam until His return. Peter tells us that we were redeemed *"With precious blood, as of a lamb unblemished and spotless, the blood of Christ"* (I Peter 1:19). Christ Jesus was the perfect sacrifice with absolutely no sin of His own. The next verse tells us, *"For He was foreknown before the foundation of the world, but has appeared in these last times for the sake of you"* (I Peter 1:20). The sacrifice of Immanuel, God with us, the only begotten Son of God, was planned before creation of the physical universe. It was planned by a loving Father who knew that we would sin and reject Him, and still He created us. Along with creating us with free will, our heavenly Father provided the way we could be brought back to Him.

We read in Romans, *"For while we were still helpless, at the right time Christ died for the ungodly. ... But God demonstrates His own love toward us, in that while we were sinners, Christ died for us. Much more then, having now been justified by His blood, we shall be saved from the wrath of God through Him"* (Romans 5:6, 8-9). We cannot redeem ourselves; as sinners, all we can do is pay the penalty. Unfortunately, the penalty is eternal separation from God.

We need to understand that God *"Desires all men to be saved and to come to the knowledge of the truth"* (I Timothy 2:4). This has always been true of God. *"Do I have any pleasure in the death of the wicked, declares the Lord God, rather than that he should turn from his ways and live?"* (Ezekiel 18:23). Of course, the answer is no.

Jesus said this: *"Then He will say to those on His left, 'Depart from Me accursed ones, into the eternal fire which has been prepared for the devil and his angels"* (Matthew 25:41). Hell was not created with us in mind, but because of our unbelief and disobedience we will wind up there. God has done everything He can to save us from His wrath which we have earned.

The Book of Hebrews was written to Jews who had converted to Christianity and now were seeking to return to the Law of Moses. The Spirit through the writer had the purpose of establishing that Christ Jesus is supreme. The editors of the Bible Visual Resource Book presented a purpose of Hebrews saying, "It shows that Christ is greater than the prophets, the angels, Moses, Joshua, and the Jewish priesthood."[2] Hebrews also shows that the sacrifice of Jesus is greater than the animal sacrifices.

Jesus through His suffering is the author of our salvation (Hebrews 2:10). *"Although He was a Son, He learned obedience from the things which He suffered. And having been made perfect, He became the to all those who obey Him the source of eternal salvation"* (Hebrews 5:8-9). Please note that salvation is connected to obedience on our part. Jesus was required to be obedient to the Father while here. That is shown especially the night of His betrayal when He prayed in the garden. Knowing what He was about to suffer, He asked His Father to do it another way. However, ever the obedient Son, Jesus did what the Father required (Matthew 26:36-44). So do not think it strange that we are required to be obedient sons and daughters.

To understand the penalty for our sins and the price for our redemption, we need to see what Jesus paid. Think on what Jesus went through from the betrayal by one of His very own to the moment of death. McKinley comments:

> This is a story of gratuitous cruelty and fiendish delight at the suffering of an innocent man. And this innocent man was God the Son. So why does Jesus have to suffer this indignity before His crucifixion? Isn't it bad enough that He will die a horrible death? Does He have to be subjected to this sickening treatment? Jesus will die to bear the penalty for the sins of His people. But He's not paying that price here as He is spat upon and smacked and taunted. So Why?[3]

BAPTISM WHAT IS IT GOOD FOR?

Yes, why? Why all the suffering and humiliation before the cross?

Jesus had been up most likely all day. In the garden that night He prayed desperately (Matthew 26:36-46, Hebrews 5:7) for God to remove the cup from Him. Even His inner circle — Peter, James, and John — could not stay awake. The mob came in the darkness led by Judas (John 18:3-12). Jesus confronted those sent by the chief priests and the Pharisees (John 8:3). He had now gone from wanting to avoid this sacrifice to being not only willing, but being in charge. Note verse 6 of John 18, *"So when He said to them, "I am He, they drew back and fell to the ground."* John's Gospel shows us that Jesus was in charge; they were able to take Him because He allowed them to. The Lamb of God was walking to His sacrifice willingly. Jesus was focused on the cross, and there was no turning back. It was time so Jesus went *"like a lamb to the slaughter."* He said to His disciples that He could have asked for *"more that twelve legions of angels"* (Matthew 26:53). He could have walked away just as He had many times before when it wasn't time for the sacrifice. For example, *"So they were seeking to seize Him; and no man laid his hand on Him, because His hour had not yet come"* (John 7:30).

They bound Jesus, and in the early hour before dawn, He was taken before Annas, the father-in-law of the high priest, then to Caiaphas, the high priest. There He was condemned by Caiaphas, the chief priests, elders, and scribes. They found Jesus guilty and they mocked, beat, blindfolded, and reviled Him. After dawn the chief priest and members of the Sadducees and Pharisees who made up the Sanhedrin formally condemned Jesus.

Then He was taken to the Roman Governor Pilate the first time. Pilate sent Jesus to Herod where Herod and his soldiers mocked Jesus and dressed Him in a royal robe. Herod then returned Jesus to Pilate. Pilate wanted to release Jesus because he had found Him innocent. But the Jewish leaders not only wanted Jesus dead; they wanted Him crucified. Pilate's approval was necessary. Pilate resisted and had Jesus scourged. Jesus was tied to a post, stripped, and beaten with a Roman scourge. The scourge consisted of many strands, each strand having sharp objects woven in. An experienced Roman soldier would have whipped Jesus' back at a slow beat. The thirty-nine lashes given to Jesus was a Jewish limit that the Romans apparently honored. Finished with that, they then jammed a woven crown of thorns on His head. Before they returned Him to Pilate, the soldiers beat Him with their hands. Pilate gave into the Jewish leaders and sentenced Jesus to crucifixion. The Roman soldiers again mocked Jesus and beat His head with the crown of thorns still on it.

The one being crucified was normally forced to carry at least the cross bar of the cross. Jesus was now clearly too physically weak to carry even just the cross bar. At the place of execution, the soldiers stripped Jesus naked. They then drove spikes into His hands or wrists, having enough play to move a little stretched out on the cross bar now attached to the upright. This was done flat on the ground. Then His feet were held one over the other as a spike was driven through them. The soldiers lifted the cross upright and dropped it into the hole.

The shock throughout His body as the cross hit the bottom of the hole must have been tremendous. Jesus' weight was now supported by the spikes through His limbs. His raw back must have caused excruciating pain as it slid down the rough wood. As He hung down, breathing was impossible because of the compression on His chest. To be able to breathe, He pushed up by straightening His knees, but as He did that, His back would been scraped along the coarse wood of the cross. This would be a continual movement pushing up, dropping down, pushing up, for six hours. The soldiers gambled under His feet for His meager clothing, and the mob made fun of Him as He suffered.

From noon until three p.m. He was in darkness, just as sinners are to be cast into the outer darkness (Matthew 8:12, 22:13, and 25:30). *"And He Himself bore our sins in His body on the cross"* (I Peter 2:24a). Jesus, symbolically had all of mankind's sins placed on Him. *"He made Him who knew no sin to be sin on our behalf"* (II Corinthians 5:21a). At the ninth hour or after being six hours on the cross, Jesus cried out, *"My God, My God, why have You forsaken Me?"* (Mark 15:34). He had a final drink of vinegar and said, "It is finished." Then He gave up His spirit (John 19:30).

Remember in the prayer that Jesus offered in the garden the night He was betrayed, *"Let this cup pass from Me"*

(Matthew 26:c). Jesus did not want to taste God's wrath, but as an obedient Son, He drank.

How does understanding that Jesus drank of the cup of the wrath of God in your place make you feel? Everything that Jesus went through was for you. All of God's wrath that you had earned because of your sin was placed on Him. Jesus, who was God John 1:1, lovingly and willingly stepped into your place to save you from the wrath you earned.

In Revelation 14:9-11 we read of the wrath of God which is pictured as a drink:

> *Then another angel, a third one, followed them, saying with a loud voice. 'If anyone worships the beast and his image, and receives a mark on his forehead or on his hand, he also will drink of the wine of the wrath of God, which is mixed in the cup of His anger, and he will be tormented with fire and brimstone in the presence of the holy angels and in the presence of the Lamb. And the smoke of their torment goes up forever and ever; they have no rest day and night, those who worship the beast and his image, and whoever receives the mark of his name.*

What is your value to God? How much does God love you? Do you understand the price that was paid on the cross to redeem you by the Son of God? Look again at all that Jesus went through from the moment He put Himself in man's hands to when He said, "It is finished."

BAPTISM WHAT IS IT GOOD FOR?

We Need The Shed Blood of Jesus

"For the life of the flesh is in the blood, and I have given it to you on the altar to make atonement for your souls; for it is the blood by reason of the life that makes atonement" (Leviticus 17:11). God told Adam and Eve that the day they ate of the tree of the knowledge of good and evil they would die. Violate God's commandment and the penalty is death. In Leviticus we see the clear connection of blood to life. Remove the blood, and life dies. Even in our culture the shedding of blood equates to death.

There is but one penalty for sin, and that is death. The price required is all the blood. Not some, but all. However, we cannot pay the penalty because we are stained by sin. Alone, without Jesus, all we could do is suffer the penalty.

John tells us that *"The blood of Jesus His Son cleanses us from all sin."* (I John 1:8c) Prior to His death at the last Passover, Jesus shared with His Disciples and said, *"This is My blood of the covenant, which is poured out for many"* (Mark 14:24b). *"Much more then, having now been justified by His blood, we shall be saved from the wrath of God through Him"* (Romans 5:9).

In the vision granted to John we read, *"Then one of the elders answered, saying to me, "These are who are clothed in the white robes, who are they, and where have they come from?" I said to him, "My lord, you know." And he said to me, "These are the ones who come out of the great tribulation, and they have washed their robes and made them white in the blood of the Lamb"* (Revelation 7:13-

14). As John said in I John 1:8, *"The blood of Jesus His Son cleanses us from all sin."*

Jesus's shed blood wipes away all trace of sin in the believer. We are then seen by God dressed in pure, spotless, white robes.

Jesus entered the heavenly tabernacle, where the Father is. *"And not through the blood of goats and calves, but through His own blood, He entered the holy place once for all, having obtained eternal redemption"* (Hebrews 9:12). Jesus purchased our redemption by offering His own blood, blood shed on the cross.

While some may not like the idea, blood is an important part of God's plan. The writer of the letter to the Hebrews builds a case for the importance of blood and the superiority of the new covenant because of the death of Jesus. Look first at how God used the blood of animals under the Old Covenant.

> *For a covenant is valid only when men are dead, for it is never in force while the one who made it lives. Therefore even the first covenant was not inaugurated without blood. For when every commandment had been spoken by Moses to all the people according to the Law, he took the blood of the calves and the goats, with water and scarlet wool and hyssop, and sprinkled both the book itself and all the people, saying, "This is the blood of the covenant which God command you," and in the same way he sprinkled both the tabernacle and all*

> *the vessels of the ministry with blood, and according to the Law, one may say, all things are cleansed with blood, and without shedding of blood there is no forgiveness* (Hebrews 9:17-22).

Under the Old Covenant all the objects used and all the people as well were cleansed by blood. Therefore, they were dedicated to God's purpose.

R. Milligan's comments on Hebrews 9:20:

> This is the blood by means of which the covenant is ratified, and you yourselves purified and consecrated to God as His peculiar people. This shows that without the shedding and sprinkling of blood, the people could not be received into covenant relation with God: nay more, that without this blood, the covenant itself could have no validity.[4]

Jesus said, *"This is My blood of the covenant, which is poured out for many"* (Mark 14:24b). The Old Covenant was inaugurated with blood of sacrificial animals, but the New Covenant was inaugurated with the superior blood of Christ Jesus. *"For it is impossible for the blood of bulls and goats to take away sins"* (Hebrews 10:4). How can an animal stand in for a human being, who is created in the image of God? The animal sacrifices were offered year after year. On the other hand, the sacrifice of the only begotten Son of God had to be offered only one time. *"But He, having offered one sacrifice for sins for all time, sat down at the right hand of God"* (Hebrews 10:12).

"In fact, the law requires that nearly everything be cleansed with blood, and without the shedding of blood there is no forgiveness" (Hebrews 9:22 NIV). It takes shed blood or death, which is the penalty for sins. We could not pay the price and have our sins forgiven because by the shedding of our blood. We are just paying the penalty. Since Jesus lived a sinless life as a man, He could pay the penalty for mankind. *"He is the atoning sacrifice for our sins"* (I John 2:2a NIV). Jesus stepped in to pay the debt that we could not pay. Without Jesus's shed blood, we would be hopelessly doomed.

"And from Jesus Christ the faithful witness, the firstborn of the dead, and ruler of all kings on earth. ***To him who loves us and has freed us from our sins by his blood"*** (Revelation 1:5 ESV). (Emphasis is mine) We are freed from our sins by Jesus' shed blood.

When Jesus instituted what is now referred to as the Lord's Supper or Communion, He said referring to the cup, *"This is my blood of the covenant, which is poured out for many for the forgiveness of sins"* (Matthew 26:28 ESV).

When was Jesus' blood poured out or shed? *"But one of the soldiers pierced his side with a spear. And at once there came out blood and water"* (John 19:34 ESV). Jesus shed His blood in death. *"Or do you not know that all of us who have been baptized into Christ Jesus have been baptized into His death?"* (Romans 6:3). Recounting his baptism, Paul said he was told, *"Rise and be baptized and wash away your sins, calling on his name"* (Acts 22:16b ESV).

A believer's past sins are washed away by the blood of Christ Jesus in baptism. This is when we connect with Christ's blood not only to cleanse our past sins, but to cleanse of sins we will commit after being raised to a new life (I John 1:7-10).

Our dead sinful nature is buried in baptism, and our new spiritual nature is raised up. When we are clothed in Jesus, we are seen clean and righteous.

CHAPTER THIRTEEN: WHY DO WE NEED JESUS?

1. F. Delitzsch, *Isaiah, Commentary On The Old Testament,* page 509.
2. *The Bible Visual Resource Book for Do-It-Yourself Bible Scholars,* Regal Books A Division of Gospel Light Publications, Ventura, California, U.S.A., 1989, page 269.
3. Mike McKinley, *Passion,* The Good Book Company, 2013, pages 43-44.
4. R. Milligan, *The New Testament Commentary, VOL. IX — Epistle To The Hebrews,* page 260.

CHAPTER FOURTEEN: HOW IS BAPTISM ADMINISTERED?

"And Jesus came to them and said, 'All authority in heaven and on earth has been given to me. Therefore go and make disciples of all the nations, baptizing them in the name of the Father and of the Son and of the Holy Spirit" (Matthew 28:18-19 NIV).

Since baptism is a command of the Lord Jesus Christ, it cannot be ignored. Paul urges the Ephesian Christians to patiently bear with one another and keep the unity of the Spirit. He gives a list of what is important to unity. There is one body or church, one Spirit, one hope, one Lord which is Jesus whom God exalted, one faith or belief system, one baptism, and one God and Father (Ephesians 4:1-6).

Paul in Ephesians is clearly making the point regarding the one baptism that it is the one in which all Christians share. That one baptism is connected with the unity of the body. As we study the early history of Jesus' church, we see that all believers were baptized. Many scholars with differing beliefs agree that there is only one definition of baptism.

W. E. Vine defines the word "Baptisma..." baptism," consisting of the processes of immersion, submersion and emergence (from baptō, "to dip").[1]

Gareth L. Reese further expands on the meaning of baptism: "Now let's pay attention to what it means to be "baptized." What action is signified by that verb? The Greek verb *baptize,* in our version transliterated "baptize" means "immerse" or "dip."[2]

Reese continues to explain:

> The word "baptize" means *immerse* in the original. One may ask any Greek working in this country and learn that simple fact. The Greek Catholic church has always known this fact and still practices immersion to this day. Jesus walked about sixty-five miles to be immersed in the Jordan River. John baptized at Aenon because there was "much" water there (John 3:23). Philip took the eunuch *"down into the water"* and both of them *"came up out of the water"* (Acts 8:38,39). Paul tells us that we are buried in baptism (Romans 6:4-6).[3]

Martin Luther in his book, *The Babylonian Captivity of the Church,* made the following statement about baptism:

> It is therefore indeed correct to say that baptism is a washing away of sins, but the expression is too mild and weak to bring out the full significance of baptism, which is
>
> rather a symbol of death and resurrection. For this reason, I would have those who are to be baptized completely immersed in the water, as the word says and as the mystery indicates. Not because I deem this necessary, but because it would be well

to give to a thing so perfect and complete a sign that is also complete and perfect. And this is doubtless the way in which it was instituted by Christ. The sinner does not so much need to be washed as he needs to die, in order to be wholly renewed and made another creature, and to be conformed to the death and resurrection of Christ, with whom he dies and rises again through baptism.[4]

From the above quote it can be seen that Luther endorsed baptism as complete immersion in water and that Jesus was the one who instituted immersion.

In the article by Rebaptdude titled *Immersion* various Bible scholars are quoted as to their connecting immersion with the original word for baptism:

> **Presbyterian**
> John Calvin -"The very word "baptize however, signifies to IMMERSE, and it is certain that IMMERSION was the practice of the ancient church."(*Institutes of the Christian Religion*, chapter 15)
> **Lutheran**
> Martin Luther -" I could wish that the baptized should be totally IMMERSED according to the meaning of the word."
> Philip Schaff -"IMMERSION and not sprinkling was unquestionably the original normal form of

baptism. This is shown by the meaning of the Greek word and the analogy of the baptism of John which was performed in Jordan." (*History of the Apostolic Church,* p. 568).

Roman Catholic

Cardinal Gibbons -"For several centuries after the establishment of Christianity baptism was usually conferred by IMMERSION; but since the 12th century the practice of baptism by infusion has prevailed in the Catholic church, as this manner is attained with less inconvenience than by IMMERSION (*Faith of our Fathers* p. 317).

Methodist

John Wesley -commenting on Romans 6:4- "We are buried with Him- alluding to the ancient manner of baptism by IMMERSION (Explanatory notes Upon the New Testament, p. 376).

George Whitefield -commenting on Romans 6:4 - "It is certain that the words of our text is an allusion to the manner of baptism by IMMERSION."

Episcopalians

Conybeare and Howson -commenting on Romans 6:4 -"This passage cannot be understood unless it is understood that the primitive baptism was by IMMERSION."[5]

What Christians follow must be backed up only by the inspired word of God rather than creeds and traditions of different groups. However, what Biblical scholars write can be a secondary source of understanding. Men's writings must be recognized as men's words and not God's words; therefore, they have no authority.

Consider the following scriptures relating to baptism:

"Surely no one can refuse water for these to be baptized..." (Acts 10:47). This verse requires water as needed to baptize. It works for sprinkling, pouring, and immersion.

"John also was baptizing in Aenon near Salem, because there was much water there..." (John 3:23). Only immersion requires much water. Sprinkling and pouring can be done with very little water.

"...and they both went down into the water, Philip as well as the eunuch, and he baptized him" (Acts 8:38). Both the one baptizing and the one baptized went down into the water. This is only required for immersion. If one is sprinkled with water or had water poured over him, there is no need to go into the water to accomplish those actions.

"When they came up out of the water..." (Acts 8:39) Philip and the eunuch. Jesus also, after His baptism, came up out of the water, *"Immediately, coming up out of the water..."* (Mark 1:10). Only immersion would need this action.

"Therefore we have been buried with Him through baptism into death..." (Romans 6:4). Being immersed

under water pictures being buried. Sprinkling and pouring would not picture a burial.

"Having been buried with Him in baptism, in which you were also raised up with Him..." (Colossians 2:12, c.f. Romans 6:4). Coming up out of being immersed under water pictures a resurrection.

When we think of the concept of being buried as put forth in the Scriptures, being laid under water is a perfect symbol of that action.

A.H. Strong discusses baptism in length and gives the reasons that baptism is administered by immersion:

> 2. *The Mode of Baptism.* This is immersion, and immersion only. This appears from the following considerations: A. The command to baptize is a command to immerse — We show this: (a) From the meaning of the original word $\beta\alpha\pi\tau\iota\zeta\omega$. That this is to immerse, appears: First, — from the usage of Greek writers — including the church Fathers, when they do not speak of the Christian rite, and the authors of the Greek version of the Old Testament ... Secondly, — every passage where the word occurs in the New Testament either requires or allows the meaning immerse ... (d) From the figurative allusions to the ordinance ... (e) From the testimony of church history as to the practice of the early church ... (f) From the doctrine and practice of the Greek church ... The prevailing

> usage of any word determines the sense it bears, when found in a command of Christ. We have seen, not only that the prevailing usage of the Greek language determines the meaning of the word 'baptize' to be 'immerse,' but that this is its fundamental constant, and only meaning. The original command to baptize is therefore a command to immerse.[6]

Augustus Hopkins Strong studied the original word and the usage of secular Greek writers of antiquity and the church fathers of the first centuries of the church age, and his conclusion was that baptism was accomplished only when the candidate was immersed.

We see from the scriptures above regarding baptism that much water is necessary; going down in the water, and coming up out of the water strongly show that baptism is immersion. Therefore, the only acceptable mode of baptism is that the candidate is fully put under water and raised up out of the water.

The original word, βαπτίζω, pronounced "baptizo," was not translated into English; it was transliterated. It was brought over into the English language as *baptize*. Scholars debate as to why this was done rather than translate the Greek using *immerse*. When we look at the historical accounts, we find that by the time the Scriptures were translated into English, sprinkling, pouring, and immersion were all being used by various groups. It might mean that the translators did not want to challenge anyone.

The importance is that this is one of the major dividing points hindering unity.

Some argue that the one baptism in Ephesians Four is the fact of baptism, but not the mode. Hence, sprinkling, pouring, and immersion all would be acceptable. The problem is that the writers and those originally reading the letters understood that the mode of baptism is immersion. Just because man changes things later does not mean God endorses that change.

"There is one body and one Spirit, just as also you were called in one hope of your calling; one Lord, one faith, one baptism, one God and Father of all who is over all and through all and in all" (Ephesians 4:4-6). There is only one baptism according to the Scriptures. The only baptism that fits what is in the New Testament Scriptures is immersion.

CHAPTER FOURTEEN: HOW IS BAPTISM ADMINISTERED?

1. *Vine's Expository Dictionary of Biblical Words, A Complete Expository Dictionary of the Old And New Testaments in One Volume,* Editors: W.E. Vine, Merrill F. Unger, and William White, jr., Thomas Nelson Publishers, Nashville, Camden, New York, 1985. Page 50 of An Expository Dictionary of New Testament Words with their Precise Meanings for English Readers.
2. Gareth L. Reese, *New Testament History A Critical and Exegetical Commentary on the Book of Acts,* page 75.
3. Ibid, page 75.
4. C.M. Sheffield, Puritan Board, https://www.puritanboard.com/threads/*Luther:Immersion the Best Mode of Baptism.97883/.*, April 15, 2019, Martin Luther, *The Babylonian Captivity of the Church.*
5. Rebaptdude, Puritan Board, https://www.puritanboard.com/threads/*immersion-questions.34598/.*, July 19, 2008,
6. Augustus Hopkins Strong, *SYSTEMATIC THEOLOGY,* pages 933 through 938.

CHAPTER FIFTEEN
WHAT THE CHRISTIAN WRITERS OF THE FIRST, SECOND, AND THIRD CENTURIES SAY ABOUT BAPTISM

The Christian writers of the early centuries — the first, second, and third — have provided a wealth of documents as to the practice of the church then. While they are not inspired as the actual men that God chose to communicate were, their writings contain valuable insight as to the practices of the Lord's church. Warren Wilcox, a former instructor at the Bear Valley Bible Institute, said in a class on Christian Evidences in 1976, "We can reconstruct the New Testament from their letters if all the ancient manuscripts were destroyed with only minor non-doctrinal omissions." Therefore, I am including quotes from their documents in this study.

F. W. Mattox said concerning the early Christian writers: "The uninspired writers who did their work from the year 100 to 150 A.D. are generally referred to as the Apostolic Fathers. These are the men who knew the Apostles or knew people who had known them and had received their teaching in this direct manner."[1]

BAPTISM WHAT IS IT GOOD FOR?

A.D. 100 to 150

The Epistle of Barnabas or simply *Barnabas*. J.B. Lightfoot says, "Possibly its author was some unknown namesake of the 'Son of Consolation.'"[2] Lightfoot gives the date of the epistle between A.D. 70 and A.D. 132.[3]

"*Barnabas:* Blessed are those who placed their hope in his cross and descended into the water ... We descend into the water full of sins and uncleanness, and we ascend bearing reverence in our heart and having hope in Jesus in our spirit (11:1, 8, 11)."[4] This writing pictures a going down into water and coming up out of it.

The Shepherd of Hermas or ***The Shepherd***. Lightfoot references the two titles connected with this work.[5] "The date is uncertain. The work is found in general circulation in the Eastern and Western Churches, soon after the middle of the second century."[6] More recent critics place the date around 90-100 A.D.[7]

Hermas could have been the one who knew the apostle Paul around A.D. 58 (Romans 16:14). He could have been the brother of Pius I, A.D. 140-155 or another Hermas around A.D. 90-100.[8]

"*Hermas, Shepherd:* ... Your life was saved and will be saved through water. ... we descended into the water and received forgiveness of our former sins. ... They descend then into the water dead and they ascend alive."[9]

The Didache or ***Teaching Of The*** **Apostles** as Lightfoot identifies the two titles used.[10] Mattox states that the author is unknown and the date is around 150 A.D or earlier.[11]

"***Didache:*** Concerning baptism, baptize in this way. After you have spoken all these things, "baptize in the name of the Father, and of the Son, and of the Holy Spirit," in running water. If you do not have running water, baptize in other water…"[12] The Didache connects what Jesus said, *"Baptizing them in the name of the Father and the Son and the Holy Spirit,"* with the use of water.

Apology written 150 A.D. Author was Justin Martyr A.D. 103-165 and the work is dated around 150 A.D.[13]

Justin: "As many as are persuaded and believe that the things taught and said by us are true and promise to be able to live accordingly are taught to fast, pray, and ask God for the forgiveness of past sins, while we pray and fast with them. Then they are led by us to where there is water, and in the manner of the regeneration by which we ourselves were regenerated they are regenerated. For at that time they obtain for themselves the washing in water in the name of God the Master of all and Father, and of our Savior Jesus Christ, and of the Holy Spirit. For Christ also said, "Unless you are regenerated, you cannot enter the kingdom of heaven."[14] Justin is referencing John 3:3. He connects regeneration with forgiveness of sins, water, and in the name of Father, Son, and Holy Spirit."

BAPTISM WHAT IS IT GOOD FOR?

A.D. 185 to 250

Against Heresies by Irenaeus, written about 185 A.D. Mattox tells us that Irenaeus was born about 130 A.D. and died around 200 A.D.[15]

Irenaeus: "Now, this is what faith does for us, as the elders, the disciples of the apostles, have handed down to us. First of all, it admonishes us to remember that we have received baptism for remission of sins, in the name of God the Father, and in the name of Jesus Christ, the Son of God, who became incarnate and died and was raised, and in the Holy Spirit of God; and that baptism is the seal of eternal life and is rebirth unto God, and that we be no more children of moral men, but of the eternal and everlasting God, (*Proof of the Apostolic Preaching 3*)
For so (they said) do the faithful keep when there abides constantly in them the Holy Spirit, who is given by Him in baptism. (*Ibid. 42*)."[16]

Tertullian: "Baptism itself is a bodily act, because we are immersed in water, but it has a spiritual effect, because we are set free from sins. *(On Baptism 7")*[17]. Mattox informs us that Tertullian was born around 155 A.D.[18]

Origen (in commenting on the crossing of the Red Sea speaks of Christian Baptism): The evil spirits seek to overtake you, but you descend into the water and you escape safely; having washed away the filth of sin, you come up a "new man," ready to sing the "new song."

(Homilies on Exodus V:5)[19]. Mattox says that Origen was born in 185 A.D.[20]

Cyril of Jerusalem: "For as he plunges into the waters and is baptized is surrounded on all sides by the waters, so were they also baptized completely by the Spirit. *(Catechetical Lectures XVII:14')*[21] "Cyril (born about 315 A. D., and made Bishop of Jerusalem in 350 A. D.)'[22]

These are just a few examples of the early Christians citing baptism as immersion. These men include students of the apostles of Jesus. Clearly immersion was the accepted means of baptism for the first four centuries after Jesus ascended back to the Father.

Ferguson studied the writings of the Apostolic Fathers and he said, "THE EFFICACY of baptism in bringing the remission of sins was not questioned, hence many put off baptism as long as possible, lest such a powerful act be wasted before one's life of sin was over."[23]

It is important to understand that baptism from the beginning has been connected with the forgiveness of sins.

Ferguson says in summing up his chapters in *Early Christians Speak,* "The ordinary practice of baptism in the ancient church was immersion. Such is the consistent testimony of the sources from the New Testament until later times."[24]

We have the examples of the early church that they considered baptism to be immersion in water and that it is connected with having sins removed. Should we not follow that rather than accept what man has changed to over the centuries?

When Did Baptism Change from Immersion?

We need to consider sprinkling and how it started. Mattox provides information on how sprinkling came about:

> Sprinkling for baptism was accepted during this period only on an emergency basis. Baptism throughout this period was recognized as necessary for the remission of sins and for salvation. Since many unbaptized would become seriously ill and immersion seemed unwise, the priests poured water on the subject's head and called it baptism. The first known case of this was Novation in 251. What was introduced as an exception later became the rule.[25]

Stephen Beale writes in an article concerning Jerome's translation of the Bible:

> **3. Baptism.** One of the challenges of the Latin translator is the many Greek words for which there is no analogue in Latin. Sometimes Jerome, or his forbearers, Latinized it.
>
> Sometimes an adequate substitute was found. Baptism is one of the Greek words apparently deemed so important that it was Latinized rather than translated. In Greek, the word is βαπτίζω,

pronounced *baptizó*. This passed over into Latin with virtually no phonetic change: *baptizo*.[26]

Jerome made the translation, *Latin Vulgate,* in the fourth century, 382 A.D., having been commissioned by Pope Damasus I.[27]

Cotham provides a little more on the change from immersion to sprinkling. "But in A.D. 1311, the Council of Ravenna, in Italy, made sprinkling *legal* as baptism to any one, whether sick or not."[28]

A council of men decided to change immersion to sprinkling or even pouring. It is clear from the examples from Scriptures given in Chapter Fourteen of this study that the first-century Christians practiced immersion. In this Chapter we have seen that the early church fathers considered baptism to be accomplished by immersion. Romans Chapter Six shows that baptism pictures a burial and a resurrection.

The question that we must face is, does man have the right, authority, or power to change what Jesus, who has all authority in heaven and on earth, said? Do we have the right to change the original meaning of a word from the way it was used and understood in the Scriptures at the time of their writing, especially one connected with salvation? In the study of the Scriptures and the writings of the early church fathers and later scholars, it is clear that the meaning of the Greek word for *baptism* is *immersion*. Therefore, changing the meaning to mean what wasn't originally meant cannot be acceptable.

CHAPTER FIFTEEN: WHAT THE CHRISTIAN WRITERS OF THE FIRST, SECOND, AND THIRD CENTURIES SAY ABOUT BAPTISM

1. F.W. Mattox, *The Eternal Kingdom: A History of the Church of Christ,* Revised and With Additional Chapters, John McRay, Gospel Light Publishing Company, Delight, Arkansas, 1961, pages 55-56.
2. J.B. Lightfoot, *The Apostolic Fathers,* Edited and Completed by J.R. Harmer, Baker Book House, Grand Rapids, Michigan, 1974, page 134.
3. Ibid, page 134.
4. Everett Ferguson, *Early Christians Speak Faith and Life in the First Three Centuries,* Revised Issue, ACU Press, Abilene Christian University, Abilene, Texas, 1987, page 33.
5. Lightfoot, page 159.
6. Ibid, page 161.
7. Ibid, page 162.
8. Ibid, pages 161, 162.
9. Ferguson, *Early Christians Speak Faith and Life in the First Three Centuries,* page 33.
10. Lightfoot, page 121.
11. Mattox, page 62.
12. Ferguson, *Early Christians Speak Faith and Life in the First Three Centuries,* page 34.
13. Mattox, page 68.
14. Ferguson, *Early Christians Speak Faith and Life in the First Three Centuries,* page 34.

15. Mattox page 78.
16. Ferguson, *Early Christians Speak Faith and Life in the First Three Centuries,* page 35.
17. Ferguson, *Early Christians Speak Faith and Life in the First Three Centuries*, page 45.
18. Mattox, page 82.
19. Ferguson, *Early Christians Speak Faith and Life in the First Three Centuries,* page 45.
20. Mattox, page 85.
21. Everett Ferguson, *CHURCH HISTORY, EARLY AND MEDIEVAL Second Edition,* Biblical Research Press, 1966, page 38.
22. Francis Joseph Winder, *That They May Be Won,* Restoration Reprint Library, College Press, Joplin, Missouri, reprint of the 1950 edition, page 102.
23. Ferguson, *Early Christians Speak Faith and Life in the First Three Centuries*, page 38.
24. Ibid, page 47.
25. Mattox, pages 150-151.
26. Stephen Beale, *7 Ways St. Jerome's Vulgate Helped Shaped the Church,* https://catholicexchange,com, September 30, 2015.
27. https://en.wikipedia.org/wiki/Vulgate
28. Perry B. Cotham, *Conversion,* published by Perry B. Cotham, 1976. Page 115.

CHAPTER SIXTEEN
BORN AGAIN

Nicodemus, a Pharisee who was also a ruler of the Jews, came to Jesus at night. Nicodemus acknowledged that Jesus was from God because of the signs or miracles that Jesus did (John 3:1-2). It seems that Jesus' response is completely unrelated to what Nicodemus said. *"Truly, truly, I say to you, unless one is born again he cannot see the kingdom of God"* (John 3:3b).

Nicodemus, completely misunderstanding, equates what Jesus said with being physically reborn (John 3:4). My paraphrase of what Nicodemus said, "Come on, you don't really expect a grown man to re-enter his mother's womb again and go through the birth canal again. That's really dumb."

"Jesus answered, 'Truly, truly, I say to you, unless one is born of water and the Spirit he cannot enter into the kingdom of God. That which is born of the flesh is flesh, and that which is born of the Spirit is spirit. Do not be amazed that I said to you, 'You must be born again'" (John 3:5-7).

Being born again is a requirement of Jesus for anyone to see or become part of God's kingdom. Jesus is stating the fact that without a rebirth one cannot enter the kingdom of heaven. By the double use of *truly, truly* there is no question that a rebirth is absolutely necessary. There are two elements involved in the concept of being born again. Water and the Spirit are the two required elements.

The washing away of their sins done by God followed by receiving the Holy Spirit from God. The Holy Spirit then enables the person to walk in the newness of life. Walking in newness of life is walking with God. Beasley-Murray on being born, again explains:

> If Nicodemus would be born anew, he must be baptized on repentance and faith in the word of the Kingdom preached by its herald, John the Baptist, and its representative, the Son of Man. That is the first thing. A second follows: he must know the life of the Spirit, for entrance to the Kingdom is ministered by the Spirit. In the proclamation of John these two things were separated as prophecy and a hope of fulfillment, since the baptizer in water was one and the baptizer Spirit another. On the lips of Jesus they come closer, as a promise 'in sure and certain hope' of fulfillment, for the baptism is from Him who shall baptize with Spirit. This baptism of the Spirit is not to be postponed until the end of all things; it awaits the 'lifting up' of the Son of Man on the cross, and thence in the presence of the Father, after which the Spirit is given and life in Christ becomes a reality (Jn, 3:14f, 7:39). Then the baptism commanded by Him will be a baptism in Spirit — a being born of water and Spirit.[1]

BAPTISM WHAT IS IT GOOD FOR?

In continuing the dialogue of Jesus with Nicodemus we read, *"That which is born of the flesh is flesh, and that which is born of the Spirit is spirit"* (John 3:6). Dods says, "The necessity of the new birth is further exhibited by a comparison of the first and second birth."[2]

In order to have physical life, we have to undergo a physical birth. Likewise, to have a spiritual life we must undergo a spiritual birth. When we undergo the process of being born again, we are sinless just like we were when we came out of our mother's womb.

To really be born again of the Spirit, one must know the reason for that action and the change in relationship that happens. Hebrews 8:7-13 shows us that in the New Covenant we know about God and Christ first, as opposed to the Old Covenant in which people were in the Covenant before they knew anything about God.

We are reminded in Titus that we do not earn salvation; it is given by God because of His mercy and grace. *"But when the kindness of God our Savior and His love for mankind appeared, He saved us, not on the basis of deeds which we have done in righteousness, but according to His mercy by the washing of regeneration and the renewing of the Holy Spirit"* (Titus 3:4-5).

We cannot gain salvation by good deeds, or any works, or rite that is man's duty. From the moment of our first sin we are under sentence of death, which is eternal separation from God. Simply put, the debt that we now owe because of even one sin, we cannot pay for our debt is our very life, and we have nothing to satisfy that debt. All we can do is to suffer the penalty.

Titus 3:4-5 connects the washing of regeneration and having the Spirit to God's action. Jesus in John 3:5 couples water and the Holy Spirit together for a new, cleansed life. Grace comes into play as Paul tells us that our righteous deeds do not save us.

McCurley reminds us:

> Just as we become a member of our physical family through physical birth, we become a member of our spiritual family through spiritual birth. God's family consists of those who have been washed in the blood of Christ and saved from the burden of sin, and the only way to have that blessing is to be born again.[3]

The concept of being born again can be understood as a change of state. Brents says, "A birth contemplates a change of state — a transition or passing from one state to another. A change of state, then, and the beginning of a new life, is the thought conveyed by the expression "born again."[4]

> *But when the fullness of time had come, God sent forth His Son, born of woman, born under the law, to redeem those who were under the law, so that we might receive adoption as sons. And because you are sons, God has sent the Spirit of his Son into*

> *our hearts, crying, "Abba! Father!" So you are no longer a slave, but a son, and if a son, then an heir through God* (Galatians 4:4-7 ESV).

When we are born again, we pass from being without God to a being a child of God. The relationship that was broken by sin is restored through the process of being born again. This is only possible because of Jesus going to the cross and dying for mankind.

See SPECIAL STUDY A8 "WHAT DO THE WORDS WATER AND THE SPIRIT IN JOHN 3:5 MEAN?" for help in understanding the two words used in connection with the rebirth.

CHAPTER SIXTEEN: BORN AGAIN

1. G.R. Beasley-Murray, page 230.
2. Marcus Dods, *The Gospel of St. John, The Expositor's Greek New Testament,* edited by W. Robertson Nicoll, D.D., Grand Rapids Book Manufacturers, Inc., Grand Rapids, Michigan, 1974, page 714.
3. Chris McCurley, *The Church Cherishes The Plan Of Salvation,* 2012 Bear Valley Lectures, *What's Right With The Church,* edited by Neal Pollard, A Publication of the Bear Valley Bible Institute of Denver, printed by Sheridan Books, Inc., 2012, page 114.
4. T.W. Brents, *The Gospel Plan of Salvation,* Gospel Advocate Company, Nashville, Tenn., 1973 Sixteenth Edition, page 196.

CHAPTER SEVENTEEN
ROMANS SIX: A DEEPER LOOK

Romans Chapter Six follows a statement made in Romans 5:20, *"But where sin increased, grace abounded all the more."* Romans Six begins, *"What shall we say then? Are we to continue in sin so that grace may increase?"* The more we sin the more grace is available! "Wow, I can," as the saying goes, "have my cake and eat it too." However, Romans 6:2 quashes that idea with *"May it never be!"* The King James translation says, *"God forbid!"* Paul gives the reason for not continuing in sin, *"How shall we who died to sin still live in it?"* (Romans 6:2b). Beasley-Murray comments on Romans 6:1ff:

> *Let us carry on in sin that grace may abound!" (Rom 6:1). He (Paul) could have countered with a purely theoretical consideration: 'Under no circumstances! Such conduct would frustrate the intention of grace.' Instead he appealed to an event in the past on which it would be unthinkable to go back: 'We died to sin once; how can we live in it still?' (Rom. 6:2)*[1]

Jesus tells us that *"No one, after putting his hand to the plow and looking back, is fit for the kingdom of God"* (Luke 9:62). Once we have committed to Jesus, we must not go back to the old life. Our commitment to Jesus must be real, it must be firmly held on to, and the cost must be counted before making a commitment. Jesus plainly warns those who would follow Him that their very family could turn against them. He gave two examples, one a man starting to build a tower who cannot finish it because of not having enough money, and he was ridiculed. The other is a king going to war finding out the enemy outnumbered him twenty to one (Luke 14:25-33). Jesus also warns us that Christians will be hated just as He was, and His followers will be persecuted.

It is unfair to teach people about Jesus and not prepare them for what it can and will cost them. Read the letters to the seven churches in Revelation 2:1-3:22, and look at what those who overcome will receive. Consider the price Jesus paid to redeem the faithful and to offer redemption to all of humanity. Is eternal redemption worth it?

A fully surrendered will and complete submission to God's will is what is required. A changing of being in control to submitting to Jesus is necessary. We are slaves to what controls us. What God has decreed is not negotiable. The author of Hebrews reminds us that Jesus made a new covenant (Hebrews 9:15). *"For a covenant is valid only when men are dead, for it is never in force while the one who made it lives"* (Hebrews 9:16). Therefore, with Jesus' death the means of salvation is set. Speaking of Jesus, Peter and John said, *"Salvation is found in no one else, for there is no other name under heaven given to men by which we must be saved"* (Acts 4:12, NIV). Jesus said that He is the only means of coming to the Father (John 14:6).

BAPTISM WHAT IS IT GOOD FOR?

For those who are capable of understanding right from wrong, there are only two states. One is to be a slave of righteousness and the other is to be a slave of sin. There is no middle ground.

Paul explains in Romans 6:12-19 that we were once slaves to sin and obeyed the lusts of sin, but now we are slaves of righteousness. We are under grace and not law-keeping. Therefore, our lives are now obedient to God and not our physical nature. We live God-governed lives, not sin-governed lives. That does not mean that we are perfect in resisting sin, but that we strive in resisting a lifestyle of sin. As John wrote, *"If we say that we have no sin, we are deceiving ourselves and the truth is not in us. If we confess our sins, He is faithful and righteous to forgive us our sins and to cleanse us from all unrighteousness"* (I John 1:8-9). When we sin, we must acknowledge it honestly and ask our Father for forgiveness, and He will grant forgiveness freely.

We are dead to a lifestyle of sin. When did we die? *"Or do you not know that all of us who have been baptized into Christ Jesus have been baptized into His death? Therefore we have been buried with Him through baptism into death, so that as Christ was raised from the dead through the glory of the Father, so we too might walk in newness of life"* (Romans 6:3-4). *"Knowing this, that our old self was crucified with Him, in order that our body of sin might be done away with, so that we would no longer be slaves to sin; for he who has died is freed from sin"* (Romans 6:6-7).

When do we die? We die to our selfish nature when by our faith, repentance, and commitment we submit to being baptized into Christ Jesus, and in so doing, we join His death. Just being baptized does not link me with Christ Jesus. We must have faith in God, in His promises, in what Jesus did on the cross, trust and accept His grace, and commit our life to His rule.

Being symbolically buried in water in order to be united with Jesus' death is an interesting concept. We understand that we bury only those who are dead. However, Romans 6 clearly says that we are buried through baptism into death. On the cross Jesus died physically and in so doing, He paid the redemptive price so that the Father can forgive sins. We must think of death as separation. We come to baptism with the desire and commitment to have our sinful nature, which is our fleshly lifestyle, put to death. We want to start living a spiritual life, which is the life we were created to live.

Regarding dying to sin, McGuiggan writes:

> Those people died to sin when they entered into union with Jesus Christ. This dying to sin involves the whole process of becoming Christ's. It speaks of the sinner's own renunciation of sin, his being immersed into union with Christ and it presupposes the rising into newness of life.... Paul is stressing the ethical necessities involved in being trustingly immersed into Christ. His immediate aim is clear.

BAPTISM WHAT IS IT GOOD FOR?

He wishes to make the point that people who died to sin can't logically continue to live in it.[2]

Jesus died on the cross and satisfied God's wrath. He was dead when buried and made alive when resurrected. Consider carefully the following illustration. A person hears the Gospel, believes, understands that he needs to repent or turn from his sinful life, appeals for a clean conscience, acknowledges Jesus as Savior and Lord, then through immersion is buried and united with the result of Jesus' death. Like Jesus, he is raised up to new life. When a person reaches the point of being baptized, he says, "I am separating myself from a sinful life, and I am determined to die to a self-governed life." Paul put it this, *"It is no longer I who live, but Christ lives in me"* (Galatians 2:20b). As Christ gave His life for me, I give my life to Him for His use and purpose.

If Jesus had died, was buried, and wasn't resurrected, then He would have been just another prophet who was slain, a martyr. Read Acts 2:14-36, which tells about the first time the Gospel message was proclaimed. Note that the message centers around the resurrection of Jesus. Some of those people hearing that Jesus was alive saw the crucifixion, and they knew He was dead; but many had been hearing He was seen alive. The resurrection declared with certainty that Jesus was God's promised Messiah and Lord (Acts 2:36). After seeing Jesus alive, Thomas acknowledged Him as his Lord and his God (John 20:28). Because Jesus rose from the dead, we know that when we come up out of the water, we now have a new life. Thanks to our Lord and our God, our life is clean and righteous because of being united with Christ Jesus.

The new life that we have because we died is now hidden with Christ in God (Colossians 3:3). We are dressed in His righteousness, for we have none of our own. Now when we sin, we can ask for forgiveness, and God will forgive us (I John 1:8). Our new life is one that is centered on Jesus and not on fleshly desires.

To have a meaningful baptism, we must acknowledge that we have sinned and that we need to be reconciled to God. We must understand that we are separated from God. In Christ we have a new clean standing with the Father God. That relationship with the Father is available only to those who are in Christ.

"Therefore if anyone is in Christ, he is a new creature; the old things passed away; behold new things have come. Now all these things are from God, who reconciled us to Himself through Christ" (II Corinthians 5:17-18b).

Consider also, *"For you are all sons of God through faith in Christ Jesus. For all of you who were baptized into Christ have clothed yourselves with Christ"* (Galatians 3:26-27).

Hendriksen writes:

The apostle is speaking, therefore, not about the merely outward administration of baptism, as if some magical healing power adhered to it, but about *the sign and seal in conjunction*

with that which is signified and sealed. All those, then, who by means of their baptism have truly laid aside, in principle, their garment of sin, and have truly been decked with the robe of Christ's righteousness, having been buried with him and raised with him, having put on Christ (cf. Rom. 6:3ff; 13:14; Col, 2:12, 13).[3]

The baptized believer has been dressed in Christ's righteous life which He lived and exhibited as He walked among mankind. Being in Christ signifies that the believer is united with Him. Therefore, if a person is not in Christ there is no relationship, and the benefits of being united with Christ are non-existent.

Strong speaks of union with Christ: "(c) Union with Christ gives to the believer the legal standing and rights of Christ. As Christ's union with the race involves *Justification*. The believer is entitled to take for his own all that Christ is."[4]

Union with Christ makes us fellow heirs of God and sharers of His glory (Romans 8:17). Being united with Him makes us righteous before God (II Corinthians 5:21). We have eternal life through that union (I John 5:11-13). Those are but a few blessings of what unity with Christ Jesus gives us.

Strong continues, "(d) Union with Christ secures to the believer the continuously transforming, assimilating power of Christ's life."[5]

As we read in Romans 6:3 and Galatians 3:27, we are baptized into Christ Jesus. Also, Galatians 3:27 states that we have clothed ourselves with Christ in baptism. Romans 13:14a says, *"But put on the Lord Jesus Christ."* Paul said this, *"For to me, to live is Christ"* (Philippians 1:21a). We are to develop a Christ-like attitude (Philippians 2:5). If we are looking at Jesus, that is, studying Him, and as we submit to Him, we will become more and more like Him (II Corinthians 3:18). Our thoughts should conform to His thoughts (II Corinthians 10:5).

*Or do you not know that all of us who have been baptized into Christ Jesus have been baptized into His death? Therefore we have been buried with Him through baptism into death, so that as Christ was raised from the dead through the glory of the Father, so we too might walk in newness of life (*Romans 6:3-4).

J.W. McGarvey makes the statement:

> We were buried with him, through immersion, unto death as to our sin: that like as Christ was raised from the dead, because of the glory of the just and holy Father required it, so we also might walk or act in a new manner of life; i.e., a sinless life. Thus baptism, which is a burial and resurrection performed in water, attests, in the strongest manner, the Christian's obligation to be sinless.[6]

BAPTISM WHAT IS IT GOOD FOR?

Immersion clearly pictures a burial and a resurrection. Immersion is a visual representation that a death to a life governed by sin has taken place and that there is a resurrection to real life in Christ. Christ now is who governs the born-again believer. When the believer understands and makes the commitment to put self and a life of sin behind, he then is ready to be baptized committing to Jesus as Lord of his life. Based on Romans 6, how can we say that simply believing in Jesus grants us the new birth? Only in baptism are we united with Christ Jesus.

Consider what F. F. Bruce says on the importance and place of baptism in the believer's conversion:

> Listen, he (Paul) says, 'do you not remember what happened when you were baptized?' From this and other references to baptism in Paul's writings, it is certain that he did not regard baptism as an 'optional extra' in the Christian life, and that he would not have contemplated the phenomenon of an unbaptized believer'.[7]

"Therefore we have been buried with Him through baptism into death, so that as Christ was raised from the dead through the glory of the Father, so we too might walk in newness of life" (Romans 6:4).

As Christ was raised from the dead, we are raised from a life dead to God unto a new life. We live a life now that is God led and committed no longer to be a slave to our old sinful nature. Our life is now united with our Father.

"Knowing this, that our old self was crucified with Him, in order that our body of sin might be done away with, so that we would no longer be slaves to sin; for he who has died is freed from sin" (Romans 6:6-7).

Baptism on our part is a demonstration of our willing obedience and a submission to the Father's will. Like Paul we now say, *"I have been crucified with Christ; and it is no longer I who live, but Christ lives in me; and the life which I now live in the flesh I live by faith in the Son of God, who loved me and gave Himself up for me"* (Galatians 2:20).

I now have a new life, a new mindset. *"Therefore if you have been raised up with Christ, keep seeking the things above, where Christ is, seated at the right hand of God. Set your mind on the things above, not on the things that are on the earth. For you have died and your life is hidden with Christ in God"* (Colossians 3:1-3). Since I have been raised to a new life my mindset needs to be focused on godly things and not worldly things. *"... we are taking every thought captive to the obedience of Christ"* (II Corinthians 10:5b).

Being Dead

As Romans Chapter Six tells us, we join Christ Jesus' death when we are baptized. We need to consider the concept of being dead. This is important to fully grasp the idea of what it means to be buried with Christ and raised to a new life in Christ.

BAPTISM WHAT IS IT GOOD FOR?

We reach a point when we can understand right from wrong. The age of accountability, as some call it, is when we are held responsible for our actions. We are held accountable for our first sin by God, and we are now separated from Him and dead in our trespasses. We are convicted of our sins and know that we are dead to God. Because of our hearing and believing we repent, confess, and are baptized. We are then raised up and are given the new real life in Christ. Thus, we are now dead to the call of our fleshly nature.

In writing the letter to the Ephesians, Paul reminded them, *"And you were dead in your trespasses and sins. In which you formerly walked according to the course of this world"* (Ephesians 2:1-2a). Before we really knew God and followed Him, we were as dead or separated from God as were the Ephesians. Our sins separated us from a relationship with God.

In his book *An Analysis of Sin,* Nelson Smith has a quote that is interesting; "Someone has said, 'Sin is man's declaration of his independence of God.'"[8]

We like to think that we know what is best for us. We know what will make us the happiest and give us a great life. We might have a good life here, but when you put that up against eternity, that isn't even a drop in the bucket. Our heavenly Father wants what is best for us. As Solomon said, *"There is a way which seems right to a man, but its end is the way of death"* (Proverbs 14:12).

"Behold, the Lord's hand is not so short that it cannot save; nor is His ear so dull that it cannot hear. But your iniquities have made a separation between you and your God, and your sins have hidden His face from you so that He does not hear" (Isaiah 59:1-2). Because of our sins we are cut off from God.

Nelson Smith writes, "However, the worst of all consequences deriving from sin is that it brings death spiritually! And it does this immediately! Sin immediately alienates us from God. Separates us from Him! ... This separated condition Paul calls death ... (Ephesians 2:1)."[10]

Outside of Christ you may be walking around; however, in God's eyes you are separated from Him and seen as being dead. There is nothing that we can do to negate the penalty. *"The wages of sin is death"* (Romans 6:23a). In Ezekiel God says, *"The soul who sins will die"* and *"The person who sins will die"* (Ezekiel 18:4 and 20). The minute we sin by violating God's commandments, even unknowingly, we stand condemned. God gave Adam and Eve one simple thing that He forbade them to do. He promised in the day that they violated that commandment, they would die. They did sin, and that very day they were cast away from the garden, and God no longer walked with them. Their sin condemned them to separation from God, and the penalty was immediately carried out. We cannot do enough, pray enough, or obey enough to pay the penalty, even if we had all of eternity to work and pray. We were without hope, lost because of our personal sins.

BAPTISM WHAT IS IT GOOD FOR?

"For while we were still helpless, at the right time Christ died for the ungodly. ... But God demonstrates His own love toward us, in that we were yet sinners, Christ died for us" (Romans 5:6-8). There is hope!

Consider the letter to the Colossians concerning Christ Jesus,

> *For in Him all the fullness of Deity dwells in bodily form, and in Him you have been made complete, and He is the head over all rule and authority; and in Him you were also circumcised with a circumcision made without hands, in the removal of the body of the flesh by the circumcision of Christ; having been buried with Him in baptism, in which you were also raised up with Him through faith in the working of God, who raised Him from the dead. When you were dead in your transgressions and the uncircumcision of your flesh, He made you alive together with Him, having forgiven us all our transgressions* (Colossians 2:9-13).

The points made in Colossians 2:9-13:

- Jesus was God with us in the flesh.
- In Jesus we are complete.
- Christ Jesus has all authority.
- In Jesus we were circumcised, a spiritual circumcision in which our fleshly nature was removed.

- We were buried with Him in baptism or immersion.
- We were raised up with Him.
- The raising up was done by God which we accepted because of our faith in God because God proved He can resurrect us by resurrecting Jesus.
- We had been dead.
- God has made us alive together with Christ.
- All our transgressions are forgiven.

The story we call the Prodigal Son in Luke 15:11-32 is a good illustration of death as separation and a returning to the Father resulting in life. *"But we had to celebrate and rejoice, for this brother of yours was dead and has begun to live, and was lost and has been found"* (Luke 15:32). *"I tell you, there is joy in the presence of the angels of God over one sinner who repents"* (Luke 15:10b). When someone turns back to God, there is great rejoicing. Just like we rejoice when a baby is born, God and His angels rejoice each time someone is raised up out of baptism to begin a new life. They rejoice because that person has begun to live.

Alive in Christ

"I came that they may have life, and have it abundantly" (John 10:10). Bruce, in commenting on John 10:10-13 says, "He desires and promotes their wellbeing: he is not content that they should eke out a bare and miserable existence; he wants them to live life to the full."[11]

Remember that without being in Christ we are dead (Ephesians 2:1). Christ Jesus brings us not just life, but abundant, full, and real life which is only life that is lived reconciled with God as He meant us to live when He created us.

"And the testimony is this, that God has given us eternal life, and this life is in His Son" (I John 5:11). Real life is only in Jesus, the Son of God.

The life that we are talking about is explained by W.E. Vine:

> zōē ... is used in the NT "of life as a principle, life in the absolute sense, life as God has it, that which the Father has in Himself, and which He gave to the Incarnate Son to have in Himself, John 5:6 and which the Son manifested in the world, I John 1:2.[12]

This is the real life that God, our Creator, decreed for us, and the life that Jesus makes available to us. *"Even when we were dead in our transgressions, made us alive together with Christ, (by grace you have been save"* (Ephesians 2:5). Weed says:

> Paul emphasizes man's culpability for his situation of alienation from God and God's rightful wrath toward mankind. Yet Paul also stresses that the act of deliverance is totally God's doing, proclaiming his might in **mercy** and **love.** God **made us alive** clearly indicates God as the source of deliverance,

also specifying that believers are already delivered (Col. 1:13, cf. I Peter 1:3). More specifically, the apostle refers to the readers' baptism as the point at which they were incorporated into Christ and empowered by God (see 5:14, Col. 2:12, 20; 3:1ff.).[13]

Consider the following quote by Strong:

> A truly baptized person is one who has passed from the old world into the new …. The water rolls over his person, signifying that his place in nature is ignored, that his old nature is entirely set aside, in short, that he is a dead man, that the flesh with all that pertained thereto — its sins and its liabilities — is buried in the grave of Christ and can never come into God's sight again …. When the believer rises up from the water, expression is given to the truth that he comes up as the possessor of a new life, even the resurrection life of Christ, to which divine righteousness inseparav attaches.[14]

"Therefore if anyone is in Christ, he is a new creature; the old things passed away; behold new things have come" (II Corinthians 5:17). When we are in Christ, we are new and clean. God promises under the New Covenant to never remember our forgiven sins (Hebrews 8:12b).

Coffman writes about the phrase "in Christ" which Paul uses 169 times:

BAPTISM WHAT IS IT GOOD FOR?

> Failure to appreciate what Paul means by this is to misunderstand everything. Paul has just written that all men are dead spiritually, a deadness that shall never abate unless they are risen again *in Christ.* In Christ, a new spiritual life is given to the convert; in Christ, all of his previous sins are cancelled; in Christ, he is endowed with the Holy Spirit; in Christ, a new and glorious life begins; in Christ, old values are rejected, old standards repudiated, and old lusts are crucified; in Christ, are "all spiritual blessings" (Eph. 1:3); out of Christ, there is nothing but death, remorse, hopelessness and condemnation; in Christ, there is the life eternal![15]

The new life is found only in Christ. Therefore, the great question that we are concerned about should be, "How do I get in Christ?"

Consider the following Scriptures:

Romans 6:3 *"Or do you not know that all of us who have been baptized into Christ Jesus have been baptized into His death?"* We are baptized into Christ!

Galatians 3:27 *"For all of you who were baptized into Christ have clothed yourselves with Christ."* Baptism is into Christ.

I Corinthians 12:13a *"For by one Spirit we were baptized into one body, whether Jews or Greeks, whether slaves or free, and we were all made to drink of one Spirit"*

Speaking of Christ Colossians 1:18a tells us, *"He is also head of the body, the church."* We are also baptized into Christ's body, which is His church. Understand that submission to Christ through baptism not only unites us with Him, but it also unites us with His church.

If we haven't been baptized, that is, immersed into Christ's death, if we haven't been baptized into Christ Himself, if we aren't clothed with Christ, and if we haven't been united with His church, then we are still dead. If we haven't been baptized, how can we say that we are united with Christ Jesus? We must understand that outside of Christ Jesus there is NO REAL LIFE!

Howard puts it this way, "There can be no mistake about it! The baptism of a believing, penitent person, who has confessed his faith in Christ, is that baptism of a person who experiences the transition — **"into Christ."**[16]

Baptism into Christ marks a changed social relationship. There are two aspects that are pictured — for the candidate, a seeking to be right with the Father; and for the Father, an acceptance. Jesus illustrated it with the Prodigal Son. The son leaves his father, lives his life pleasing himself, sinks to the depths of despair, admits his sins, and seeks to return in full humility, not even seeking the relationship that he had before. The father, upon seeing his lost son returning, runs to accept him back into the family as a son. There is no rubbing his son's sins in his face, only loving acceptance (Luke 15:11-32). This story pictures God accepting the repentant person.

BAPTISM WHAT IS IT GOOD FOR?

God's grace offered through Christ Jesus gives us a new clean, spotless, and forgiven life based on the sacrifice of God's Son. Not only that but, we are seen as righteous by God's standard because we have Jesus' perfect life clothing us. Thus, our broken relationship with the Father is restored.

CHAPTER SEVENTEEN: ROMANS SIX: A DEEPER LOOK

1. G.R. Beasley-Murray, page 143.
2. Jim McGuiggan, *The Book of Romans, Looking Into The Bible Series,* Montex Publishing Company, Lubbock, Texas, 1982, page 191.
3. William Hendriksen, *Galatians, Ephesians, Philippians, Colossians, and Philemon,* page 149.
4. Augustus Hopkins Strong, *Systematic Theology,* page 805.
5. Ibid, page 805.
6. J.W. McGarvey and Philip Y. Pendleton, *The Standard Bible Commentary Thessalonians, Corinthians, Galatians, and Romans,* page 343.
7. F. F. Bruce, *The Epistle Of Paul To The Romans,* page 136.
8. Ibid, page 136.
9. Nelson Smith, *An Analysis of Sin,* page 21.
10. Ibid, page 27.
11. F.F. Bruce, *The Gospel of John,* page 226.
12. *Vine's Expository Dictionary of Biblical Words, A Complete Expository Dictionary of the Old And New Testaments in One Volume,* Editors: W.E. Vine, Merrill F. Unger, and William White, jr., Thomas Nelson Publishers, Nashville, Camden, New York, 1985, page 367 of *An Expository Dictionary of New Testament Words with their Precise Meanings for English Readers.*
13. Michael R. Weed, *The Letters of Paul to The Ephesians, the Colossians, and Philemon,* The Living Word Commentary, editor Everett Ferguson, R.B. Sweet Co., Inc., Austin, Texas, 1971, page 136.

14. Augustus Hopkins Strong, *Systematic Theology,* page 941.
15. James Burton Coffman, *Commentary on 1 and 2 Corinthians,* page 372.
16. V. E. Howard, *New Testament Conversions.* Central Printers and Publishers, West Monroe, Louisiana, 1980, page 14.

CHAPTER EIGHTEEN
WASHING OUR ROBES

"Blessed are those who wash their robes, so they have the right to the tree of life, and may enter by the gates into the city. Outside are the dogs and the sorcerers and the immoral persons and the murders and the idolaters, and everyone who loves and practices lying" (Revelation 22:14-15).

What exactly does Jesus mean by saying, *"Blessed are those who wash their robes"*? We have seen that we are clothed in Christ in this study. Therefore, how do we fit into the concept of grace the idea of washing our robes? The idea of washing our robes implies action or work on our part.

In the vision John sees a group in white robes, and one of the elders asks John who they are (Revelation 7:9, 13). *"I said to him, "My lord, you know." And he said to me, "These are the ones who come out of the great tribulation, and they have washed their robes and made them white in the blood of the Lamb"* (Revelation 7:14). They have washed their robes in the blood of Christ.

A benefit of having robes washed white in the blood of Christ is that those with white robes have the right to the tree of life (Revelation 22:14). Those whose robes are washed are in contrast with the sinners. The prophet Isaiah wrote what God said, *"Though your sins are as scarlet, they will be as white as snow; though they are red like crimson, they will be like wool"* (Isaiah 1:18).

McGuiggan says of those who have washed their robes, "Here the point stressed is the person's going to Jesus rather than what Jesus can do for him."[1] These verses in Revelation chapters 7 and 22 speak of the individual's commitment to Jesus as Lord.

B.W. Johnson comments: "WHITE — To be clothed in white is to be innocent, pure, and to be triumphant"[2]

Consider, *"He saved us, not on the basis of deeds which we have done in righteousness, but according to His mercy, by the washing of regeneration and renewing by the Holy Spirit"* (Titus 3:5).

Brents writes concerning Titus 3:5:

> He saved us how? By the washing of regeneration and renewing of the Holy Ghost. What is this washing of regeneration? It cannot be the renewing of the Holy Ghost, for that is specifically mentioned. The Spirit and the water are not the same, for "there are three that bear witness in earth, the Spirit, and the water, and the blood." I John verse 8. Then, if the washing of regeneration is not baptism, what is it?[3]

The Apostle Paul, speaking of his conversion, quoted what Ananias said: *"Now why do you delay? Get up and be baptized, and wash away your sins, calling on His name"* (Acts 22:16).

Saul, later to be called Paul, met Jesus on the road to Damascus. Jesus struck Saul blind. Meeting Jesus caused Saul to believe in Him. He obeyed Jesus by doing what he was told to do. Jesus sent Ananias to tell Paul what he needed to do (Acts 9:1-19 and 22:6-16).

In Paul's statement in Acts 22:16, we note that he was told to be baptized. Reese says that "Be baptized" literally means "cause yourself to be baptized."[4] Reese goes on, "Baptism is connected with the washing away of sins. This verse is strongly indicative of the fact that a man's sins are not forgiven in God's mind until the time the man is obedient in baptism."[5]

It is clear that our sins committed prior to being baptized are not washed away before baptism. Remember that without belief, acknowledging and repenting of our sins, confessing Jesus as Lord and Savior and obedience, baptism is a meaningless action or rite.

In I Corinthians 6:9-10 Paul reminds the Corinthians of who they were before they came to Christ Jesus. They were sinners, and as such excluded from heaven. Then Paul says, *"Such were some of you; but you were washed, but you were sanctified, but you were justified in the name of the Lord Jesus Christ and in the Spirit of our God"* (I Corinthians 6:11). Beasley-Murray comments on verse 11:

BAPTISM WHAT IS IT GOOD FOR?

> The coincidence of language between 'you had yourselves washed ... in the name of the Lord Jesus Christ' and that used by Ananias to Paul, 'Get baptized and wash away your sins, calling on his name' (Acts 22:16) is so close as to make it difficult to dissociate the 'washing of I Cor. 6:11 from the baptismal cleansing.[6]

We are washed or cleansed of our sins by the blood of Jesus which first occurs when we are baptized. However, this is not a onetime cleansing consider what John wrote to believers:

> *This is the message we have heard from him and proclaim to you, that God is light, and in him is no darkness at all. If we say we have fellowship with him, while we still walk in in darkness, we lie and do not practice the truth. But if we walk in the light, as he is in the light, we have fellowship with one another, and the blood of Jesus his Son cleanses us from all sin. If we say we have no sin, we deceive ourselves, and the truth is not in us. If we confess our sins, he is faithful and just to forgive our sins and to cleanse us from all unrighteousness.* (I John 1:5-9 ESV).

Those who are in Jesus will sin, but if they are following Him, they will know that they have sinned and will with godly sorrow repent, confessing their sin, and the Father will forgive. If Christians choose not to be honest and confess their sins, they cannot be forgiven. Continual following Jesus and admitting it when sin is committed enables the robes to be cleansed.

Calling on The Name of Jesus

"And there is salvation in no one else; for there is no other name under heaven that has been given among men by which we must be saved" (Acts 4:12).

"For the Scripture says, "Whoever believes in Him will not be disappointed." For there is no distinction between Jew and Greek; for the same Lord is Lord of all, abounding in riches for all who call on Him; for "Whoever will call on the name of the Lord will be saved" (Romans 10:11-13).

In the name of Jesus and only in His name is there salvation. Jesus was given all authority in heaven and on earth (Matthew 28:18). Because Jesus emptied Himself and became like us and was obedient by dying on the cross, God highly exalted Him. Everyone in heaven, on the earth, and under the earth will bow to Him and will confess that Jesus is Lord (Philippians 2:6-11). Even though He begged the Father to save Him from death, He obeyed the Father, and He is now the source of eternal life (Hebrews 5:7-9). Jesus is exalted, praised, and glorified because He submitted to the Father's will and plan.

When we call on the name of Jesus, we are admitting that we are helpless and that we are unable to save ourselves. We are reminded that we were helpless, but that Christ died for the ungodly (Romans 5:6). We are the ungodly ones before we are baptized. McGuiggan, in commenting on Romans 10:13, says:

> To be baptized in his name (Acts 2:38) is to be baptized upon his authority. To be baptized "into" the name of the Father, Son, and Holy Spirit (Matthew 28:19) is to be baptized into union with the Godhead. To do what we do in the name of Christ (Colossians 3:17) is to act remembering who he is and what he stands for. To believe on his name (John 1:12; 2:23; 3:18) is to believe on him. To call upon his name (Acts 22:16; Romans 10:13) is to beg him for aid and salvation. This implies one's needy condition.[7]

We must realize our need of Christ to want His help and His redemption and to accept it.

Consider what the Apostle Peter wrote about Noah and his family who were *"brought safely through the water"* (I Peter 3:20) and his comparison to baptism. *"Corresponding to that, baptism now saves you — not the removal of dirt from the flesh, but an appeal to God for a good conscience — through the resurrection of Jesus Christ"* (I Peter 3:21).

Noah and his family were saved not by being in the ark, but through the water. The water at the time of Noah removed the influence of evil and cleansed the earth. In like manner, baptism now saves us, not the physical washing of our bodies. Our sins and evil nature are spiritually removed.

The NASB calls baptism *an appeal*. Other words used in various translations are: *interrogation of, mark of, request, answer of, examination, demand, and asking of*. The Greek Dictionary in *The New American Standard Exhaustive Concordance of The Bible* gives this definition: "**1906.** ἐπερώτημα **eperōtēma:** from 1905; an inquiry, a demand: — appeal (1).[8]

When we are baptized, it is not for the purpose of washing our bodies, that is, the outside. Connected with baptism we learn there is an appeal for a good conscience. N. T. Caton, commenting on I Peter 3:21, explains:

> Toward God the answer of the conscience is good whenever our own conscience assures us that we have done just what God requires of us. ... God commands baptism. Man complying has a conscience in that respect void of offense. His conscience is good. It could not have been good had he failed to obey the command.[9]

When we submit and are baptized, we know exactly when we obeyed and committed fully to the Lord. We have the assurance that all our past sins are removed and forgotten by our heavenly Father.

Let us couple calling on the name of Jesus with the obedient submission shown in baptism, which becomes an appeal to God for a forgiven and guiltless conscience. All this is based on the fact that Jesus died, was buried, raised again, and given total, absolute authority in the physical and spiritual realms. Therefore, Jesus and only Jesus offers salvation by the Father's decree, *"God has made Him both Lord and Christ"* (Acts 2:36b).

Being praised and given glory is in store for all those who call on His name and remain faithful to the end. Consider these inspired words of Peter: *"In this you greatly rejoice, even though now for a little while, if necessary, you have been distressed by various trials, so that the proof of your faith, being more precious than gold which is perishable, even though tested by fire, may be found to result in praise and glory and honor at the revelation of Jesus Christ"* (I Peter 1:6-7). Like Jesus, we will be honored because we lived our lives in submission to the Father's will.

CHAPTER EIGHTEEN: WASHING OUR ROBES

1. Jim McGuiggan, *The Book of Revelation,* International Biblical Resources, Lubbock, Texas, 1967, page 339.
2. B.W. Johnson, *VISION OF THE AGES,* Gospel Light Publishing Company, Delight, Arkansas, page 357.
3. T.W. Brents, *The Gospel Plan of Salvation,* pages 525-526.
4. Gareth L. Reese, *New Testament History A Critical and Exegetical Commentary on the Book of Acts,* page 362.
5. Ibid page 362.
6. G.R. Beasley-Murray, page 163.
7. Jim McGuiggan, *The Book of Romans,* page 311.
8. Robert L. Thomas, Th. D., General Editor, *New American Standard Exhaustive Concordance of The Bible,* The Lockman Foundation, Holman, Nashville, Tennessee, 1980, Greek Dictionary, page 1650.
9. N. T. Caton, *A Commentary and an Exposition of the Epistles of James, Peter. John, and Jude,* The Restoration Library, Gospel Light Publishing Company, Delight, Arkansas, page 100.

CHAPTER NINETEEN
COMMITMENT

We read about a time when Jesus was heading to Jerusalem with His disciples and others. *"As they were going along the road, someone said to Him, 'I will follow You wherever You go.' And Jesus said to him, 'The foxes have holes and the birds of the air have nests, but the Son of Man has nowhere to lay His head.' And He said to another. 'Follow Me.' But he said, 'Lord, permit me first to go and bury my father.' But He said to him, 'Allow the dead to bury their own dead; but as for as for you, go and proclaim everywhere the kingdom of God.' Another also said, 'I will follow You, Lord; but first permit me to say good-bye to those at home"* (Luke 9:57-61). Jesus' answer was, *"No one, after putting his hand to the plow and looking back, is fit for the kingdom of God"* (Luke 9:62).

When Jesus committed to the Father's plan in the garden that fateful night, He made a commitment to each and every one of us (Hebrews 5:7-10). God the Father's commitment is seen in *"For God so loved the world, that He gave His only begotten Son"* (John 3:16a and Romans 5:6-10).

F. LaGard Smith's book, *Baptism The Believer's Wedding Ceremony,* speaks of baptism as a commitment like marriage. I realize that for many people today, commitment in marriage is no longer considered necessary. However, godly marriage is an example of what God intends. Throughout the Word, God's relationship with His people is pictured as a marriage relationship. God was always faithful to His "spouse," even when His people weren't faithful to Him. In the New Testament Christians are pictured as the bride of Christ. Paul, in writing to the church in Corinth, said, *"For I am jealous for you with a godly jealousy; for I betrothed you to one husband, so that to Christ I might present you as a pure virgin"* (II Corinthians 11:2). In Ephesians 5:25-33 the relationship between Jesus and the church is like that of husband and wife.

Like marriages that last only a brief season, some people become Christians and turn away from Him. One wedding I attended had the words, "As long as our paths stay the same." To me there was no real commitment made by that couple. They started out with a "get out clause" in their relationship.

A problem that can happen is the ceremony becomes the focus. In a marriage between a man and a woman the ceremony can center around a lavish and costly production. Baptism can center around the rite rather than its purpose of unity with Christ and salvation.

F. LaGard Smith points out:

> Lest we focus too closely on the ceremony itself, it is important to remind ourselves that
>
> the essence of baptism is found in the committed love relationship with Christ. In marriage of course, it is the relationship itself that brings the couple to the point of a wedding ceremony. And it

> is that same relationship that continues through the years to mature and to draw the couple closer and closer in spiritual unity.[1]

We need to grow more like Jesus as we mature spiritually. There is a lot said in Ephesians 5:22-33 regarding the relationship of Christ and His church using the human marriage union. We read, *"For this reason a man will leave his father and mother and be united to his wife, and the two will become one flesh. This is a profound mystery — but I am talking about Christ and the church. However, each one of you also must love his wife as he loves himself, and the wife must respect her husband"* (Ephesians 5:31-33 NIV).

While we read that the husband leaves his parents, the same can be said of the wife. Just as she leaves parents, we leave the world and our self-centered life to be united with Christ.

S.D.F. Salmond has this to say about the mystery of Ephesians 5:31-33:

> What immediately follows is the writer's own way of putting the matter just stated, or his own application of the words of Scripture. The sense, therefore, is this — "the truth of which I have spoken, the relation of husband and wife as one flesh, is a revelation of profound importance; but let me explain that, in speaking of it as I have done, my meaning is to direct your minds to that higher relation between Christ and His Church.[2]

Smith points out that our relationship with Christ grows from the beginning moment of our being joined with Him:

> That process of spiritual adhesion is true of baptism as well. It is one's faith relationship with Christ that brings the believer to the point of the wedding ceremony of baptism. But more important than this exciting beginning is the *spiritual growth* of the relationship we have with Christ.[3]

Just as husband and wife become one, so do those who are Christ's become one with Him. We are encouraged to have Christ's self-sacrificial attitude. *"Each of you should look not only to your own interests, but also to the interests of others. Your attitude should be the same as that of Christ Jesus"* (Philippians 2:4-5 NIV). In Second Corinthians 3:18 we learn that we are being transformed to look like Jesus.

Two words in Ephesians 5:33 help us understand the relationship between Christ and His church that the husband and wife relationship illustrates. The first is *love,* and it is addressed to husbands. The Greek word *agapō* carries the understanding that the husband in a godly healthy marriage is to love his wife like he wants to be loved, and it is a steadfast, sacrificial zeal that seeks the true good of another. *"Husbands, love your wives, just as Christ loved the church and gave himself up for her"* (Ephesians 5:25 NIV).

The wife is to respect her husband, which is the second important part of the relationship illustrating the marriage bond with Christ and His bride the church. The Greek word for *respect* used is *phobeō* in the original. A direct translation would be *fear or dread*. However, I believe that the idea is more of respect.

Hendriksen considers that *phobeō* is best translated as follows:

> The rendering "respects" is probably the best one. In our English language "fear" (A.R.V.) is somewhat ambiguous. Though it may not be a *wrong* translation, for the verb *fear* can be employed in the sense of reverencing (A.V. "reverence), nevertheless since, because of popular usage this word so easily conjures up visions of awe, dread, and fright.[4]

While Jesus calls us brothers and friends, we must remember that He is Creator, Savior, Redeemer, King, and God. We must be obedient, quick to obey, show respect, and take what He says seriously. Because Jesus was obedient to death on the cross, the Father has *"Exalted him to the highest place and gave him the name that is above every name, that at the name of Jesus every knee should bow, in heaven and on earth and under the earth"* (Philippians 2:9-10).

A problem that we can have is to think of Jesus as only our brother or friend. While those are true, Jesus Himself makes that relationship conditional. *"You are my friends if you do what I command"* (John 15:14 NIV). Regarding Christ being our brother, Paul wrote, *"For those God foreknew he also predestined to be conformed to the likeness of his Son, that he might be the firstborn among many brothers"* (Romans 8:29 NIV). God set things up before creation that those who are the redeemed are to look like Jesus. God is saying that our behavior and thinking are to be like those of His Son. Second Corinthians 3:18 says that we are being transformed to his likeness or image. We are His friends and brothers, for we willingly make His goals ours. We freely surrender our will to the Lord Jesus.

Jesus may be our older brother with all the rights of the firstborn, but He is also King of kings and Lord of lords. If we forget this and focus on brothers as equals, then we are in rebellion.

As we learn about the Father's love and our not having a relationship with Him when we are in sin, we are also learning that the Father loves us so greatly that He sent His Son to stand in our place so that we can have a restored relationship with God. We come to understand what Jesus has done for us.

The old wedding vows contained these words of commitment: "Forsaking all others, for better or worse, in sickness and health, rich or poor, until death do we part." Marriage is a covenant between a man and a woman to become one and to walk through life together. Marriages will have ups and downs, but there is always the commitment to work through things to keep that bond together. Likewise, our relationship with Christ has a demonstrated commitment for each one of us. He loves us

BAPTISM WHAT IS IT GOOD FOR?

so much that He took our punishment, He paid the penalty for us, and He redeemed us. Therefore, when we come to Him, our commitment needs to match His. As in marriage of a man and a woman, there will be ups and downs on our part, and we need to be willing to work on maintaining our relationship with Jesus.

One of the most important things is that when we reach the point of submitting by being baptized, we enter the relationship with the mindset of determination to keep that relationship intact. We will do anything to be faithful to our commitment. Jesus promises that nothing in life that happens to us, no sickness and no temptation is so strong that He cannot help us overcome, and no persecution will be able to remove us from Him as long as we hold to and honor the relationship we have with Him. In fact, Jesus warns us that we may lose family and friends, and we will suffer persecution and illness. He encourages us to remain faithful to Him. To help us He strengthens us, gives us the Spirit, and promises to be with us. He loves us with a love beyond what we see in the world, and He desires our faithful love in return. Jesus laid down the bottom line for our demonstrated love, *"If you love me, you will obey what I command"* (John 14:15 NIV). The apostle John reminds us of what Jesus said, *"And this is love: that we walk in obedience to his commands"* (II John 6 NIV).

CHAPTER NINETEEN: COMMITMENT

1. F. LaGard Smith, *Baptism: The Believer's Wedding Ceremony,* page 108.
2. S.D.F. Salmond, *The Epistle to the Ephesians,* The Expositor's Greek Testament, Volume Three, edited by W. Robertson Nicoll, Wm. B. Eerdmans Publishing Company, Grand Rapids, Michigan, 1974, page 374.
3. F. LaGard Smith, *Baptism: The Believer's Wedding Ceremony,* page 108.
4. William Hendriksen, *Galatians, Ephesians, Philippians, Colossians, and Philemon,* page 257.

CHAPTER TWENTY: IN CONCLUSION

Baptism must not be viewed as simply a "rite" that saves by itself. Baptism is meaningless without belief, obedience, and commitment on the part of the one being baptized. Baptism for the believer is a demonstration of faith or trust in God's promise by which the believer has access to and is cleansed by the saving blood of Christ Jesus. Baptism is where the believer receives the gift of the Holy Spirit, the Comforter and Helper. Baptism is the final step in asking for and receiving forgiveness of sins offered by God's grace. While grace is a free gift, we cannot fault God for setting down the conditions for accepting His grace. By offering His only begotten Son, He has extended the offer of reconciliation to us. God hates what we are without Him and offers freely a way to be reconciled.

It might appear in this book that if you do five steps, you will be redeemed. However, we cannot be saved by approaching salvation in a mechanical way. We cannot check off this list: hear √, believe √, repent √, confess √, and be baptized √. Ok, I checked all off, so God owes me salvation. Salvation is by grace and not by checking off each step as a magic formula. Yet, those five steps are the natural progression in accepting God's offer of grace.

The beginning hearing the gospel, which results in belief. Conviction of the fact of your being a sinner leads to repentance. Then you must acknowledge Jesus as Lord and Savior. You obey by being immersed, and your sins are washed away and you are clothed in Christ Jesus. If your mindset has not changed from a self-centered one to a God-centered one, there is no salvation in just doing a ritual.

Grace can be a strange concept to some. There is a proverb which states that there is no free lunch. Yet grace is freely offered, and we are to accept it freely. The acceptance of grace involves faith or trust. We must know who the Father and Jesus are and what Jesus did and why He went to the cross. We then can understand God's free gift, and we can take hold of it.

To Sum Up Baptism

Baptism is vital to acceptance into God's family, to having sins removed completely, and to having unity with Christ Jesus. It is not a simple act or a meaningless one. Therefore, I have listed what happens in baptism and what we then have as a result of baptism.

- When we submit to baptism, we pledge to serve God (I Peter 3:21).
- Being baptized into Christ removes our past sins (Acts 2:38; 22:16).
- We are clothed with Christ (Galatians 3:27). God sees us dressed in Christ's righteousness. Note that the righteousness we have comes from Christ, and we have none of our own.
- We then have God's Spirit dwelling in us (Acts 2:38; John 3:5; Titus 3:5). The Spirit within

enables us to mature spiritually and develop the fruit of the Spirit (Galatians 5:22-23).
- In baptism we are fully united with Christ, His blood, death, and His life (Romans 6:3-5).
- Baptism adds us to the redeemed, the body of Christ, the church (Acts 2:47; I Corinthians 12:13). We do not join His church; God puts us into it.
- We now have access to the continual cleansing of the blood of Christ (I John 1:7). Of course, this requires an acknowledgement of our sin to God and to ourselves as well (I John 1:8).
- Only immersion pictures death, burial, and resurrection that symbolize our dying to our past sinful lives, and our unity with the sacrificial death of Jesus and our being raised to a new life in Christ Jesus (Romans 6:3-4).

Baptism Is the Final Step Leading to A New Life

As has been pointed out, acceptance of grace is a changed mindset. It begins by first hearing, either by reading God's word and discovering the truth or by being led through the word by a mature believer. This naturally leads to a belief in Christ and the individual's current standing with God as a separated, lost sinner. This in turn causes one to repent of sin that has caused that separation and turn to God. One confesses that Jesus is Lord and God. Then one makes a commitment to live for Jesus. Baptism is public. It is done usually before at least one other person and God and the heavenly host, and it shows our acceptance of Jesus as Lord and God the Redeemer. Baptism is a firm commitment to live for and to obey Jesus. As Peter wrote, *"Baptism ... an appeal to God for a good conscience"* (I Peter 3:21). When one is baptized, he is saying, "I believe in and accept Jesus as my Lord and I surrender my will to His, and in so doing, I trust His promise of complete forgiveness of all my past sins. When I am raised up out of the watery grave, I am then adopted into God's family with all the privileges and responsibilities therein (Galatians 4:5). I have a restored relationship with my God and a new life freed from slavery to sin. If I give in to temptation and sin and confess my sin, God will forgive me (I John 1:8). The Spirit through John says, *"But if anybody does sin, we have one who speaks to the Father in our defense — Jesus Christ, the Righteous One. He is the atoning sacrifice for our sins"* (I John 2:1b-2a NIV). For the one who is in Christ there is the assurance that if he acknowledges sin when he commits it and seeks God's pardon he is forgiven.

The only way to be saved is to be in Christ. The Scriptures teach that we put on Christ in baptism. One can and must believe in Christ Jesus, but one cannot believe one's self into Him. *"For all of you who baptized into Christ have clothed yourselves with Christ"* (Galatians 3:27). When because of faith and obedience and commitment you were baptized into Christ, you begin a new direction in life. Christ is put on. *"But put on the Lord Jesus Christ, and make no provision for the flesh in regard to its lusts"* (Romans 13:14). Romans Chapter Six makes it clear that we are in union with Jesus through baptism. Our old life lived for our own selfish nature has been buried, and we are raised to a life. In Christ Jesus we have the promised abundant life. We are to have the same attitude as Jesus (Philippians 2:2-8). *"Therefore be imitators of God, as beloved children"* (Ephesians 5:1).

Now consider these words of Jesus about a particular guest at a wedding feast. *"But when the king came in to look over the dinner guests, he saw a man there who was not dressed in wedding clothes,*

and he said to him, 'Friend, how did you come in here without wedding clothes?' And the man was speechless. Then the king said to the servants, 'Bind him hand and foot, and throw him into the outer darkness; in that place there will be weeping and gnashing of teeth" (Matthew 22:11-13). We see the marriage feast of the Lamb, Jesus, in Revelation 19:7-9. There the bride or church is seen dressed in *"Fine linen, bright and clean"* (Revelation 19:8b). If we are not dressed in Christ, we will be cast out away from God's presence.

We are saved by grace. Grace is based on God's desire for reconciliation which was demonstrated on the cross through the death of Emmanuel. Is it so strange that God desires a demonstration from us when we accept His grace?

All of this is a progression of a changing mind and heart. Some readily accept it, while others struggle over it. Baptism must not be something to be entered into lightly.

Without a commitment to following Jesus totally, baptism is just an act done with no benefit gained. Baptism is a firm commitment that the one being baptized is accepting Jesus as Lord, Savior, and God of his life.

Because of Jesus' love and complete obedience to the Father through His death God has made Him supreme. *"For this reason also, God highly exalted Him, and bestowed on Him the name which is above every name, so that at the name of Jesus every knee will bow, of those who are in heaven and on the earth and under the earth, and that every tongue will confess that Jesus Christ is Lord, to the glory of God the Father"* (Philippians 2:9-11). We either accept that Jesus is Lord and bow to Him now, or when we stand in God's presence at the end, we will acknowledge that Jesus is Lord and bow down. If we wait until Judgment Day, our acknowledging Jesus and bowing to Him will be as a surrendered enemy before execution.

Consider the consequence of not being in Christ Jesus. *"When the Lord Jesus will be revealed from heaven with His mighty angels in flaming fire, dealing out retribution to those who do not know God and to those who do not obey the gospel of our Lord Jesus"* (II Thessalonians 1:7b-8). There are two things that condemn us — refusing to believe in God and not accepting and obeying the gospel, which is not accepting His atoning death.

Our Creator, Father, and Redeemer wants a restored relationship with us. He wants us to repent and accept Him as Lord over our lives. God wants the joyous commitment and surrender of a bride to her husband given freely on the wedding day and leading to a lifetime of devotion and commitment. He wants us to be one with Him, remaining with Him and learning from Him. He also wants us to be united with all other baptized believers.

In baptism our heart and soul are cleansed and made alive so that we can begin a lifetime of being transformed into the likeness of Christ, which is the image mankind was created in.

We are faced with a decision. We can embrace what God has clearly ordained, or we can say, "Well, God really didn't mean what He said." Remember that the Lord Jesus commanded baptism. Throughout God's dealings with humanity, there are the two basic things that condemn — disbelief and disobedience. Those two things still condemn today.

The premise that began this study was the need for unity among believers. Baptism is a major stumbling block to unity. As I went through the Scriptures, it was very plain that the only way into a relationship with Jesus, the Spirit, and the Father is to be buried in a watery grave and raised up out of that grave to a new life in Christ. However, without hearing God's word, having faith that God is, knowing why Jesus became like us and died, understanding our need, and verbally confessing Jesus, there is no way the act of baptism will save. It all works together as steps, starting with seeking God and ending in an obedient new life in Christ

Consider II Peter 1:20-21, *"But know this first of all, that no prophecy of Scripture is a matter of one's own interpretation, for no prophecy was ever made by an act of human will, but men moved by the Holy Spirit spoke from God."* The Bible contains what God revealed to us. In the Bible we understand what we lost through our sins, what God desires of us, and what God has done through Jesus. It may seem hard to understand, but it is direct and open to our ability to learn from it. We must read the Bible with a mind that is seeking God, what He desires from us and for us.

It is important that God, our true Father, communicated to us through the Holy Word. We must have a hunger for His word. We need to echo the words Peter spoke when many turned away from Jesus. *"Lord to whom shall we go? You have the words of eternal life"* (John 6:68b).

Christ Jesus, God with us, only begotten of the Father, Messiah, Lord, and God has ordered baptism. Why do so many seek to avoid obedience?

The question that you must answer is, "Will I accept what the Scriptures teach regarding baptism and its connection to salvation?" Or when I stand before Jesus, will I dare say, "I didn't believe that You really meant what You said"?

As pointed out in the beginning of this book, the Lord Jesus prayed that all His followers be united. The base Scripture used is; *"There is one body and one Spirit — just as you were called to the one hope that belongs to your call — one Lord, one faith, one baptism, one God and*

BAPTISM WHAT IS IT GOOD FOR?

Father of all" (Ephesians 4:4-6a). A major stumbling block to achieving unity among believers is the *"one baptism"*. The rest of these verses most believers agree on.

The conclusion of this study is that immersion is the final step in accepting God's offer of grace, a submitting to the authority of the Lord Jesus. We cannot have unity with Christ Jesus or one another unless we all recognize the *"one baptism"* as the Word of God defines it and its purpose. My prayer is that all will come to the knowledge of truth and be saved.

Edward James Wittlif

SPECIAL STUDIES

BAPTISM WHAT IS IT GOOD FOR?

A1 THE NEW TESTAMENT HAS FIVE DIFFERENT BAPTISMS

Each of the five baptisms serve a distinct and different purpose.

1. JOHN'S BAPTISM – *"As for me I baptize you with water for repentance"* (Matthew 3:11a). When the Pharisees and Sadducees came to John, he admonished them to bear fruit in keeping with a repentant heart (Matthew 3:7-9). John the baptizer's purpose was two-fold – first, to call the people back to God, and second to prepare the way of the Lord. Luke records this of John prior to his birth: *"Many of the people of Israel will he bring back to the Lord their God. And he will go on before the Lord, in the spirit and power of Elijah, to turn the hearts of the fathers to their children and the disobedient to the wisdom of the righteous — to make ready a people prepared for the Lord"* (Luke 1:16-17 NIV).

John's authority came directly from God. *"There came a man sent from God, whose name was John"* (John 1:6). Thus, John is the administrator of this baptism.

John's baptism for repentance ended with Jesus' death and resurrection. It served its purpose. On the Day of Pentecost, as recorded in Acts 2, a new baptism is proclaimed. *"Peter replied, 'Repent and be baptized every one of you, in the name of Jesus Christ for the forgiveness of your sins. And you will receive the gift of the Holy Spirit"* (Acts 2:38 NIV).

John's baptism is no longer valid. Consider:

> *And it happened that while Apollos was at Corinth, Paul passed through the inland country and came to Ephesus. There he found some disciples. And he said to them. 'Did you receive the Holy Spirit when you believed?' And they said. "No. We have not even heard that there is a Holy Spirit.' And he said. 'Into what then were you baptized?' They said, 'Into John's baptism.' And Paul said, 'John baptized with the baptism of repentance, telling the people to believe in the one who was to come after him, that is Jesus.' On hearing this, they were baptized in the name of the Lord Jesus* (Acts 19:1-5 ESV).

The twelve disciples Paul met admitted that they had been baptized only with John's baptism and had not heard of the Holy Spirit. They were then baptized "In the name of Jesus." John's baptism was a call to repent looking forward to Jesus with no mention of the Holy Spirit. Therefore, John's baptism was no longer valid.

2. BAPTISM OF SUFFERING – Luke 12:50 *"But I have a baptism to undergo, and how distressed I am until it is accomplished."* Jesus is clearly referring to Himself. This statement does not apply to Him submitting to John's baptism, for it looks forward to a future event.

BAPTISM WHAT IS IT GOOD FOR?

Boles comments on Luke 12:50, "Jesus here calls His baptism a suffering; it is an overwhelming in suffering."[1]

Up until the night of His betrayal, Jesus was fixed on the Father's and His purpose of being the sacrificial Lamb of God. In the garden that night Jesus prayed three times, asking for His Father to find another way other than His death; however, He made it clear that He would accept His Father's will (Matthew 26:36-46). The Holy Spirit enlightens us concerning Jesus' suffering. *"During the days of Jesus' life on earth, he offered up prayers and petitions with loud cries and tears to the one who save him from death, and he was heard because of his reverent submission. Although he was a son, he learned obedience from what he suffered and once made perfect he became the source of eternal salvation for all who obey him"* (Hebrews 5:8-9 NIV). Peter tells us that Jesus, throughout His trial, entrusted Himself to the Father, the one who judges righteously (I Peter 2:23). Because He was obedient to death on a cross, God highly exalted His Son and made His name above all names (Philippians 2:8-11).

Jesus was the only one to undergo this baptism in which the suffering results in salvation of others. However, Jesus warned the apostles before His arrest that if He was persecuted, they will be persecuted (John 15:18-21). Jesus also warned all followers that we will be persecuted (Matthew 5:11-12). Peter tells us that because Jesus suffered, we will suffer (I Peter

2:21). We also could go through a baptism of suffering when we follow Jesus and proclaim His gospel. The difference is that our suffering will not result in the forgiveness of sins for others.

3. BAPTISM OF THE HOLY SPIRIT – John declared that Jesus would baptize with the Holy Spirit (Matthew 3:11). Jesus told His apostles that He will baptize them with the Holy Spirit in Acts 1:5. We see that the baptism of the Holy Spirit came with power on Pentecost (Acts 2:1-4).

Is what happened on Pentecost the actual baptism of the Holy Spirit? Jesus told the apostles, His chosen ones, that in a few days they would be baptized with the Holy Spirit (Acts 1:5). He was speaking to the eleven (Acts 1:2), and He made it clear that in Jerusalem they would be baptized with the Holy Spirit. After Jesus returned to heaven and before Pentecost, another was chosen by lot to take Judas' place so that there were twelve apostles again. His name was Matthias.

The first incident of being baptized with the Holy Spirit happened on the Day of Pentecost. What do we know about this baptism? Luke tells us about it in Acts 2:1-12.

When Luke wrote Acts, he did not divide it into chapters and numbered verses. That was done much later. In the last part of Chapter One, Luke is talking about the apostles only. It follows that the "they" of verse one in Chapter Two is the twelve apostles. They are together on Pentecost. *"Suddenly a sound like the blowing of a violent wind came from heaven and filled the whole house where they were sitting"* (Acts 2:2 NIV). They heard a sound like a violent wind, but not an actual wind. The apostles next *"Saw what seemed to be tongues of fire that separated and came to rest on each of them"* (Acts 2:3 NIV). The second thing was visual and looked like tongues of fire. The result: *"All of them were filled with the Holy Spirit and began to speak in other tongues as the Spirit enabled them"* (Acts 2:4 NIV).

The baptism of the Holy Spirit happened when Jesus said it would. It was physically heard, it was physically seen, and it resulted in the apostles being able to speak in other tongues. What were the other tongues? In Jerusalem there were Jews from every nation. They heard the sound and came to see. The crowd heard the apostles speaking in each one's language. The crowd could tell that these men were from Galilee by their accents and dress. The crowd wondered how these men from Galilee spoke their native languages (Acts 2:4-12). Therefore, the meaning of the word *tongue* in the Scriptures is *language*.

Is Pentecost the only time that Jesus administered the baptism of the Holy Spirit? There is one other time. Please read carefully from Acts Chapter Ten Verse One through Chapter Eleven Verse Eighteen.

In the Jewish culture there were only two ethnic or racial groups, Jew or Gentile. To understand what was happening with Cornelius, a Roman Centurion, and his family, and friends who were Gentiles, we need to remember that ethnic distinction. Jews were the circumcised and Gentiles the uncircumcised. The Jews were God's chosen people and circumcision was the sign of God's covenant with them.

Cornelius, a Roman centurion and a Gentile, had a vision from God. In the vision Cornelius was told, *"Your prayers and gifts to the poor have come up as a memorial offering before God. Now send men to Joppa to bring back a man named Simon who is called Peter"* (Acts 10:4d-5 NIV). Because of the feelings of Jews towards Gentiles, God had to prime Peter to respond to Cornelius' request.

God gave Peter a vision, which He repeated three times. The vision involved a sheet with all kinds of four-footed animals, reptiles, and birds. Peter was told to kill and eat. Peter refused all three times because the beasts were unclean and forbidden under the Law of Moses. God then said, *"Do not call anything impure that God has made clean"* (Acts 10:15b NIV). Peter was still pondering this vision when the men Cornelius sent arrived. The Spirit told Peter to go with them because He had sent them (Acts 10:19-20).

When Cornelius related to Peter why he sent for him, everything fell into place for Peter. *"Then Peter began to speak: 'I now realize how true it is that God does not show favoritism but accepts men from every nation who fear Him and do what is right'"* (Acts 10:34 NIV).

Peter was a Jew. He and other Jewish Christians went to Cornelius' house. Cornelius, in anticipation, had gathered his relatives and close friends to hear Peter's message. *"While Peter was still speaking these words, the Holy Spirit came on all who heard the message. The circumcised believers who had come with Peter were astonished that the gift of the Holy Spirit had been poured out even on the Gentiles. For they heard them speaking in tongues and praising God"* (Acts 10:44-46 NIV).

Peter and the other Jewish Christians were amazed that the Gentiles were speaking tongues. While it doesn't say the tongues were a language that Peter and the others understood, what the Gentiles were saying praised God. As you will see in the next paragraph that Peter understood what happened in Cornelius' house was the same as Peter and the other apostles experienced on Pentecost.

After baptizing Cornelius and his household, Peter returned to Jerusalem. Jewish Christians demanded to know why he, a Jew, had dealings with the Gentiles, even eating with them (Acts 11:1-3). Peter explained his vision. He told them what happened at Cornelius' house. *"As I began to speak, the Holy Spirit came on them as he had come on us at the beginning. Then I remembered what the Lord had said, 'John baptized with water, but you will be baptized with the Holy Spirit.' So if God gave them the same gift as he gave us, who believed in the Lord Jesus Christ who was I to think that I could oppose God?"* (Acts 10:15-17 NIV).

Note the similarities between Pentecost and Cornelius' house. Peter tied the events around Cornelius with Jesus' promise to baptize the apostles with the Holy Spirit. Peter also said that it happened the same way as at the beginning, referring to Pentecost. The Scripture is silent about there being a sound like a violent wind or tongues as of fire at the baptism of Cornelius and his household. The result of the Spirit baptism was that the Gentiles spoke in a language that Peter and the other Jewish Christians knew because they knew that Cornelius and the other Gentiles were praising God. In both cases, being able to speak a foreign language is the one clearly common connection with the baptism of the Holy Spirit.

Do not lose sight of the fact that Jesus is the administrator, the one baptizing with the Holy Spirit.

John the Baptist spoke of Jesus, *"I baptize you with water for repentance, but he who is coming after me is mightier than I, whose sandals I am not worthy to carry. He will baptize you with the Holy Spirit and fire"* (Matthew 3:11 ESV).

Boles writes:

BAPTISM WHAT IS IT GOOD FOR?

This prophecy of John was literally fulfilled on the day of Pentecost (Acts 2:1-4) and at the house of Cornelius (Acts 10:44; 11:15-18) with respect to the baptism "in the Holy Spirit." John does not here state that every subject of the coming kingdom would be immersed in the Holy Spirit. His prediction should be understood in the light of its fulfillment; we have only two records of the fulfillment of the baptism in the Holy Spirit. In the baptism of the Holy Spirit on these two occasions, the Holy Spirit came direct from heaven without any intervention of human agency. The baptism in the Spirit of these two groups of persons has brought blessings to all mankind; the one on Pentecost brought blessings directly to the Jews. And the one at the house of Cornelius brought blessings to the Gentiles; hence the baptism in the Holy Spirit has resulted in blessings to the entire human family.[2]

On the Day of Pentecost, Peter is the speaker who proclaims Jesus as the risen Lord and Christ to the Jews (Acts 2:14). Peter brings to the Gentiles at Cornelius' house the message of Jesus (Acts 10). If we consider the fact that Jesus gave Peter the keys to the kingdom of heaven (Matthew 16:18) and that keys are used to unlock or lock, we understand that Peter opened heaven to the Jews first and to the Gentile second. Thus, heaven is open to all humanity.

4. BAPTISM OF FIRE – See Matthew 3:11-12 for the wicked, Matthew 25:41-46, Revelation 21:8. The baptism of fire is to punish the wicked (Matthew 3:7-12). The administrator is Christ the Lord (II Thessalonians 1:6-10).

Boles states about the baptism of fire: "We conclude that the fulfillment of the prediction of the baptism in fire would be realized by the wicked when they are cast into the lake of fire. (Rev. 20:15.)"[3]

Lewis says regarding the baptism of fire:

> The context contrasts two groups immediately before and after this expression. *Fire* in verse 10 is for the burning of fruitless trees, and in verse 12 for the burning of the chaff. Since it is unlikely that the import of the word is changed in the middle expression, it is reasonable to suppose that the fire of hell — the lake of fire (Rev. 20:15) — is in view. Fire, then, is here a symbol of judgment[4]

> *God is just: He will pay back trouble to those who trouble you and give relief to you who are troubled, and to us as well. This will happen when the Lord Jesus is revealed from heaven in blazing fire with His powerful angels. He will punish those who do not know God and who do not obey the gospel of our Lord Jesus, They will be punished with everlasting destruction and shut from the presence of the Lord* (II Thessalonian 1:6-9a NIV).

It is clear that the baptism of fire refers to the final judgement and that it is a baptism we should want no part in.

5. BAPTISM COMMANDED BY CHRIST JESUS – What is called by many the Great Commission given by Jesus is a command. *"Go therefore and make disciples of all nations, baptizing them in the name of the Father and of the Son and of the Holy Spirit"* (Matthew 28:19 ESV). Jesus tells us that baptism is necessary for everyone. *"Go into all the world and proclaim the gospel to the whole creation. Whoever believes and is baptized will be saved"* (Mark 16:15-16 ESV). Those who hear the gospel and believe will be saved. The purpose of baptism is to be united with Jesus. *"Do you not know that all of us who have been baptized into Christ Jesus were baptized into his death?"* (Romans 6:3 ESV). The result is, *"We were buried therefore with him by baptism into death, in order that, just as Christ was raised from the dead by the glory of the Father, we too might walk in newness of life"* (Romans 6:4 ESV). We now have a new life hidden in Christ (Colossians 3:3). *"And Peter said to them, 'Repent and be baptized every one of you in the name of Jesus Christ for the forgiveness of your sins, and you will receive the gift of the Holy Spirit"* (Acts 2:38 ESV). Not only are our sins forgiven, but we have God's Spirit. *"Or do you not know that your body is a temple of the Holy Spirit with you, whom you have from God"* (I Corinthians 6:19 ESV). The gift of the Spirit is the indwelling of the Holy Spirit within each one who is a baptized believer. One more thing is that being baptized unites us with all other baptized believers (I Corinthians 12:12-27).[5 and 6]

While it seems confusing that in the New Testament, we find five baptisms, we can see that each one serves a distinct purpose.

A1 THE NEW TESTAMENT HAS FIVE DIFFERENT BAPTISMS

1. H. Leo Boles, *A Commentary on The Gospel by Luke,* page 263.
2. H. Leo Boles, *A Commentary on The Gospel According to Matthew,* page 84.
3. Ibid, page 85.
4. Jack P. Lewis, *The Living Word Commentary The Gospel According to Matthew Part I 1:1-13:52,* Sweet Publishing Company, Austin, Texas, 1976, page 63.

GENERAL INFORMATION USED

5. Frances Joseph Winder, *That They May Be Won,* 1950, College Press Reprint Library, page 111.
6. Gareth L. Reese, *New Testament History Acts,* page 8.

A2 CONVERSIONS AND GROWTH OF THE CHURCH IN ACTS

Rather than just mentioning a few specific cases, I am including all verses that indicate people becoming disciples or being added to the church to look at to see if there is a common thread.

Pentecost was the first time the Gospel was preached. When Peter proclaimed the death, burial, and resurrection of Jesus, the Jews who heard the message and were convicted of having crucified the Messiah asked, *"What shall we do?"* (Acts 2:37) *"Peter said to them, 'Repent and each of you be baptized in the name of Jesus Christ for the forgiveness of your sins; and you will receive the gift of the Holy Spirit"* (Acts 2:38).

They heard the gospel message regarding Jesus and were convicted of their sins. When they heard and believed, they asked what to do. They were told to repent, meaning to acknowledge their sins and turn back to God. They were told to be baptized in the name of Jesus. When they were baptized, they were promised two things, the forgiveness of their sins and the gift of the Holy Spirit.

The immediate result of the first Christians who were baptized. *"And the Lord was adding to their number day by day those who were being saved" (Acts 2:47b).*

The ones being saved were added by God to those already saved. We do not join Christ's church or His body; God puts us in there as a result of our being saved. Those who are in Christ's church are enrolled by God because He knows their heart and commitment.

The effect of Peter and John's preaching in Acts 4.
"But many of those who had heard the message believed; and the number of the men came to be about five thousand" (Acts 4:4).

These who heard the Gospel believed. The number of men in the church grew to about five thousand.

Because the apostles performed many miraculous signs and wonders (Acts 5:12).
"And all the more believers in the Lord, multitudes of men and women, were constantly added to their number" (Acts 5:14).

Those who believed in Jesus were being added to those already in the body.

Because God's word was being proclaimed.
"The word of God kept on spreading; and the number of disciples continued to increase greatly in Jerusalem, and a great many of the priests were becoming obedient to the faith" (Acts 6:7).

Obedience to the faith is mentioned, and a great many Jewish priests were obedient believers. More and more people were responding to the Gospel.

The Samaritans. *"But when they believed Philip preaching the good news about the kingdom of God and the name of Jesus Christ, they were baptized, men and women alike. Even Simon himself believed; and after being baptized, he continued on with Philip" (Acts 8:12-13b).*

The Gospel was preached with the result that those who heard and believed were baptized.

The Ethiopian eunuch. The Ethiopian was returning from Jerusalem to the court of Candace (Acts 8:27). Philip was directed by the Spirit to join the Ethiopian, who was reading from Isaiah 53. The Ethiopian asked Philip to explain who Isaiah 53 was speaking about. Philip preached Jesus to him (Acts 8:26-35). *"As they went along the road they came to some water; and, the eunuch said, 'Look! Water! What prevents me from being baptized?"* (Acts 8:36). *"And he ordered the chariot to stop; and they both went down into the water, Philip as well as the eunuch, and he baptized him. When they came up out of the water, the Spirit of the Lord snatched Philip away; and the eunuch no longer saw him, but went on his way rejoicing"* (Acts 8:37-38).

Philip preached Jesus, and the Scripture does not mention that Philip taught baptism. However, the Ethiopian saw water and asked to be baptized. They both went into the water. The result was that the Ethiopian was baptized and he rejoiced. A logical conclusion is that when Jesus is preached, baptism is part of that message.

BAPTISM WHAT IS IT GOOD FOR?

Saul's conversion. Saul was persecuting the disciples of the Lord and was on his way to Damascus to arrest the disciples there. On that road Saul met the resurrected Jesus, who confronted him. Jesus got his attention in a most dramatic way. Saul was led to Damascus because he was now blind. He waited in Damascus three days for Ananias to arrive (Acts 9:1-19). *"So Ananias departed and entered the house, and after laying his hands on him said, "Brother Saul, the Lord Jesus. Who appeared to you on the road by which you were coming has sent me so that you may regain your sight and be filled with the Holy Spirit"* (Acts 9:17).

Ananias was sent so that Saul could see again and be filled with the Holy Spirit. "And immediately there fell from his eyes something like scales, and he regained his sight, and he got up and was baptized; and he took food and was strengthened" (Acts 9:18-19). Saul was promised his sight, which he received. He was promised to be filled with the Holy Spirit. He was baptized immediately, even before breaking a three-day fast. To Saul, being baptized was extremely important.

Recounting his conversion Saul, now known as Paul, quoted Ananias as saying, *"Now why do you delay? Get up and be baptized, and wash away your sins, calling on His name"* (Acts 22:16). There are three things that Paul understood. He had to be baptized, which was connected with the washing away of his sins, and he was told to call upon the name of Jesus.

Cornelius, the first Gentle convert. In Acts 10:1-48 we read about Cornelius, a Roman centurion, who was a believer in God. He was given a vision from God and told to send for Peter. Peter also had a vision; in fact, he had the same vision three times. God was preparing Peter to accept the Gentles. As a Jew, Peter had nothing to do with Gentles. Peter went to Cornelius' house where Cornelius had assembled his relatives and close friends. While Peter was speaking, the Holy Spirit fell on the Gentles, and they spoke in tongues. The other Jewish Christians who had come along were amazed that the Holy Spirit had been poured out on the Gentiles. They were baptized in the name of Christ (Acts 10:47 – 48).

See SPECIAL STUDY: A3 CORNELIUS RECEIVING THE SPIRIT PRIOR TO BAPTISM.

Paul and Barnabas, the first missionary journey Acts 13 and 14.

Many Gentles believed (Acts 13:48). In Iconium both Jews and Gentles believed Acts 14:1. In Derbe many disciples were made after hearing the gospel (Acts 14:21). The Gospel was preached and many believed.

Paul and Silas, the second missionary journey Acts 15:36 – 18:22.

Lydia Acts 16:14-15. *"A woman named Lydia, from the city of Thyatira, s seller of purple fabrics, a worshipper of God, was listening; and the Lord opened her heart to respond to the things spoken by Paul. And when she and her household had been baptized"* (Acts 16:14-15a). Lydia already was a worshipper of God, and when Paul spoke, the Lord opened her heart. She responded and along with her household was baptized.

The Philippian Jailor Acts 16:22-34.

Paul and Silas had been arrested, beaten, and locked into stocks. They were singing and praying about midnight, and there was an earthquake. The prison doors were opened, and all the prisoners' chains fell off. The jailor, fearing the worst, was about to kill himself when Paul stopped him. The jailor asked, *"What must I do to be saved?"*

> *They said, 'Believe in the Lord Jesus and you will be saved, you and your household. As they spoke the word of the Lord to him together with all who were in his house. And he took them that very hour of the night and washed their wounds, and immediately he was baptized, he and all his household. And he brought them into his house and set food before them, and rejoiced greatly, having believed in God with his whole household* (Acts 16:31-34).

The jailer, when he saw that all were still there, asked Paul and Silas what to do to be saved. They told him and all present in his house the answer. He took care of Paul and Silas' physical needs immediately, and he and all his household were baptized. He opened his home to Paul and

Silas and fed them, and he and his household rejoiced and believed in God.

Thessalonica Acts 17:4.

"Now when they had traveled through Amphipolis and Apollonia, they came to Thessaloncia, where there was a synagogue of the Jews. And according to Paul's custom, he went to them, and for three Sabbaths reasoned with them from the Scriptures, explaining and giving evidence that the Christ had to suffer and rise again from the dead, and saying, 'This Jesus whom I am proclaiming to you is the Christ.' And some of them were persuaded and joined Paul and Silas, along with a large number of the God-fearing Greeks and a number of the leading women" (Acts 17:4). They were persuaded by the message they heard and joined Paul and Silas and became Christians.

Berea Acts 17:10-12.

They listened to Paul, but they checked out what he was saying with the Old Testament, verse 11.

"Therefore, many of them believed, along with a number of prominent Greek women and men" (Acts 17:12). Those in Berea heard Paul and checked out what he preached. Therefore, they believed what was said matched the Old Testament scriptures.

Paul at Athens Acts 17:16-34.
Paul's sermon on Mars Hill (Acts 17:22-31).

The result: *"But some men joined him and believed, among whom were Dionysius the Areopagite and a woman named Damaris and others with them"* (Acts 17:34). They believed and joined Paul.

Paul at Corinth Acts 18:7-8.
"Crispus, the leader of the synagogue, believed in the Lord with all his household, and many of the Corinthians were believing and being baptized" (Acts 18:8). Many believed and were baptized in Corinth.

Paul, the third missionary journey Acts 18:23 – 21:17.
Paul at Ephesus in Acts 19:1-7. Paul found some believers. *"He said to them, 'Did you receive the Holy Spirit when you believed?' And they said to him. 'No, we have not even heard whether there is a Holy Spirit." And he said, 'Into what then you were baptized?' And they said, 'Into John's baptism.' Paul said, 'John baptized with the baptism of repentance, telling the people to believe in Him who was coming after him, that is, in Jesus. When they heard this, they were baptized in the name of the Lord Jesus"* (Acts 19:2-5). These were believers, but with no knowledge of the Holy Spirit. In fact, they had been baptized with John's baptism. They were baptized in the name of Jesus.

Things Connected with Salvation That Are Given in The Seventeen Examples of Conversions Listed in The Book of Acts

Listed by number of times mentioned:

NINE TIMES we see that hearing the message of Christ is mentioned. Believing in Christ and being baptized are mentioned in nine of the seventeen examples.

SIX TIMES they were either added to the church, body, or were joined with the preacher.

TWO TIMES their sins were washed away, they received the gift of the Holy Spirit, and rejoiced after being baptized.

ONE TIME they checked to make sure what they heard was true to God's word, repented, were obedient to the faith, and they called on Jesus' name as the Lord open their hearts.

From these cases we can see that there are several things involved with receiving salvation. We must hear about Christ Jesus and believe in Him. Then like those in Acts 2, we learn that we are sinners, which then leads to repentance.

Seventeen cases or examples of people being saved occur in Acts. The most common cases include hearing, believing, and being baptized. One case mentions repentance, two cases connect baptism to the removal of sins, and two connect the giving of the Holy Spirit with baptism.

We need to understand that because hearing the gospel, believing in Jesus, acknowledging our sins and repenting, confessing our belief in Jesus as Lord and Savior, being baptized, receiving the Holy Spirit, cleansing of our sins, and rejoicing are not mentioned in every one of the seventeen cases does not mean that we can omit any one of these "steps."

Hearing or reading God's word, believing that it is true, and recognizing that we are sinners and separated from God are the important foundational steps. Then understanding what Jesus did and why His sacrifice is necessary adds to that foundation. We then are motivated to repent and be sorrowful for our sins. Accepting what Jesus did on the cross for us compels the action of confessing Jesus as Savior, Lord, and God. Thus, we show our loving obedience by committing our very lives to Jesus through baptism, and we receive forgiveness, the indwelling of the Holy Spirit, and a new life. We are then motivated to learn, grow, and serve.

Gus Nichols summed the incidents of salvation in his book:

Let us distinguish between what these people had to do to be saved, on the one hand, and the incidentals and circumstances which occurred in connection with their conversion. They all heard the same gospel, believed in the same Christ, repented of sin, and upon their faith in Christ were all baptized to be saved, to get into Christ, or for the remission of sins. This is what they did. Then God saved them, pardoned their sins, and made them as innocent and just in his sight as if they had never sinned in their lives. The Lord also added them to the church.[1]

When we leave out any of the progressive steps that lead to becoming a Christian, that is a committed follower of Lord Jesus, which are hearing the Gospel, believing, repentance being moved by sorrow for sins, confessing that Jesus is Lord, and being baptized, then there is no salvation.

Why Do We Need to Be Baptized?

Because It Is A Command of The Lord Jesus.

- Matthew 28:19b, *"Make disciples of all the nations, baptizing them."* Christians are ordered to baptize people from all nations. This is called the Great Commission.
- Mark 16:16a, Mark's account of the Great Commission. *"He who has believed and has been baptized shall be saved."* While this is not worded as a direct command it is linked to salvation; therefore, baptism is shown as being necessary regarding salvation.
- Acts 2:38, The ones on the day of Pentecost were told to be baptized.
- Acts 10:48, Cornelius and the other Gentles were ordered to be baptized.
- Acts 22:16b, Paul in relating his baptism quoted Ananias as saying, "Get up and be baptized."

BAPTISM WHAT IS IT GOOD FOR?

Jesus ordered baptism; Peter, and Ananias repeated Jesus's order. Therefore, it must be considered a necessary requirement. Since Jesus, who is Lord of lords and King of kings with all authority in heaven and earth orders that we are to be baptized, who are we to argue with Him? Baptism is not optional. To deny baptism is to rebel against the King of kings and Lord of lords.

In the book of Acts are two Scriptures that are important to consider regarding membership in the fellowship of believers. *"And the Lord added to their number daily those who were being saved"* (Acts 2:47b NIV). *"Nevertheless, more and more men and women were added to their number"* (Acts 5:14).

Commenting on Acts 2:47, Reese says, "No man can "join church" like he might join some human fraternal society. He must be added by the Lord. Men are added to the body of believers when they become obedient."[2]

It is important that we understand that God is the one who adds those being saved to the body because God knows our hearts and our willingness to commit to Jesus' leadership over our lives. As Paul wrote, *"I planted the seed, Apollos watered it, but God made it grow"* (I Corinthians 3:6 NIV). God is the one who recognizes who is a Christian and causes success and growth.

A2 CONVERSIONS AND GROWTH OF THE CHURCH IN ACTS

THINGS NECESSARY FOR SALVATION IN THE EXAMPLES OF CONVERSIONS IN THE BOOK OF ACTS LISTED IN 1-17

1. Gus Nichols, *Speaking The Truth In Love,* Nichols Bros. Publishing Co., Waxahachie, Texas, 1956, page 130.
2. Gareth L. Reese, *New Testament History Acts,* page 87.

A3 CORNELIUS RECEIVING THE SPIRIT PRIOR TO BAPTISM

In Acts Chapter Ten we read about Cornelius, a Roman centurion. He was a believer in God and a devout man. God sent him a vision telling him to send for Peter. Cornelius was a Gentile, and the Gospel message about Jesus was being preached only to the Jews and Samaritans at that time. God also sent Peter a vision three times and told him to go with the men that Cornelius had sent. Peter preached the Gospel to Cornelius, his family, and friends (Acts 10:1-33). This was the first time that Gentiles heard the Gospel. Peter said, *"Everyone who believes in Him receives forgiveness of sins. While Peter was still speaking these words, the Holy Spirit fell upon all those who were listening to the message"* (Acts 10:43-44).

Cornelius, his family, and his close friends had a clear manifestation of the Holy Spirit before being baptized. After seeing that God gave them the manifestation of the Spirit Peter said, *"Surely no one can refuse the water for these to be baptized who have received the Holy Spirit just as we did, can he?"* (Acts 10:47) Does this mean the Jews have to be baptized to receive forgiveness of sins and the gift of the Holy Spirit (Acts 2:38) and the Gentiles, you and me, have the gift of the Holy Spirit prior to baptism? That would make two different purposes for baptism. For the Jew, baptism leads to salvation. For the Gentile, baptism is a sign that they have the Holy Spirit.

God needed to provide a sign to the Christians who came out of Judaism, especially those who had been Pharisees, that the Gentiles are accepted to become members of God's church through baptism. *"But some of the sect of the Pharisees who had believed stood up, saying, 'It is necessary to circumcise them and to direct them to observe the Law of Moses"* (Acts 15:5). They were connecting the Old Covenant with the New. These converts were hanging on to the old traditions and the Law of Moses. Many of Paul's writings deal with Jewish Christians trying to bind circumcision and Law keeping on the Gentles. In the letter to the Galatians Paul confronts Peter, who in Acts Chapter 15 avowed equality with the Gentile Christians. Later Peter, swayed by Jewish converts who held to the idea that Gentiles were unclean, stopped eating with the Gentile believers. Peter also led others to separate from the Gentile believers.

The Council held at Jerusalem and led by James debated this question. The answer was that the Gentiles were not required to be circumcised or to obey the Law of Moses (Acts 15). Interestingly, three of the things that were laid upon the Gentiles made it possible for Jewish and Gentile Christians to eat together. The Gentile believers were to abstain from meat that had been offered to the idols, meat where the animal had been strangled, and blood. The fourth thing prohibited to Gentiles was fornication because sex was a part of the pagan worship (Acts 15:20 and 29).

On the day of Pentecost, Peter preached the first Gospel message to Jews from every nation, thus opening the kingdom to the Jewish people (Acts 2). Then in Acts Chapter 10, Peter preached the

BAPTISM WHAT IS IT GOOD FOR?

Gospel message to Gentles. We see that Jesus used Peter both times to open the kingdom to all people.

Peter, in defending his action of baptizing Gentiles back in Jerusalem, said, *"And as I began to speak, the Holy Spirit fell upon them just as He did upon us at the beginning. And I remembered the word of the Lord, how He used to say, 'John baptized with water, but you will be baptized with the Holy Spirit.' Therefore if God gave to them the same gift as He gave to us also after believing in the Lord Jesus Christ, who was I that I could stand in God's way?"* (Acts 11:15-17).

Commenting on Acts 11:15, Reese writes:

> The reference in the word '*beginning*' is to the day of Pentecost, Acts 2; and the '*us*' is limited to the apostles. It is strongly implied that there had been no common reception of the baptism with the Holy Spirit since Pentecost, for if it were something that all Christians were expected to and did receive, Peter could have simply pointed to the numerous other incidents and did not have had to go back to Pentecost for an example.[1]

Beasley-Murray says on the Holy Spirit falling on the Gentiles prior to baptism:

> A clue as to the way we are intended to interpret the event may be seen in the astonishment of the Judaistic Christians at the manifestation of the Spirit in these Gentiles (10.45f) and the indication

in Peter's speech that he, too, felt helpless before such a sovereign act of God (11:17). His question, 'Who was I to be able to hinder God?' shows that Peter interpreted the divine action as revealing God's acceptance of Cornelius and his company and the divine pleasure that they be baptized and so enter the Church of the Messiah.[2]

God clearly conveyed the message that Gentiles were able to enter Jesus' church. They could therefore be taught and baptized and did not have to be circumcised to become a convert to the Law of Moses first.

Beasley-Murray further states:

> In that case the gift of the Spirit without baptism must be viewed as exceptional, due to a divine intervention in a highly significant situation, teaching that Gentiles may be received into the Church by baptism even when they have not removed their uncleanness through circumcision and sacrifice (11:18).[3]

"Surely no one can refuse the water for these to be baptized who have received the Holy Spirit just as we did, can he? And he ordered them to be baptized in the name of Jesus Christ" (Acts 10:47 – 48a). That Cornelius and those with him had received the Spirit does not mean that they were in Christ or forgiven of their past sins. If they had been, then baptism would not have been necessary.

BAPTISM WHAT IS IT GOOD FOR?

Reese says concerning Peter's defense in Jerusalem Acts 11:15;

> The inference also can be drawn that the 'baptism of the Holy Spirit' was not the thing that converted people, for Peter could have shown that the conversion of Cornelius was like the case of any other person who came to Christ to prove his point.[4]

As Peter said at the opening of his speaking to Cornelius and the others, *"I most certainly understand now that God is not one to show partiality, but that in every nation the man who fears Him and does what is right is welcome to Him"* (Acts 10:1b-2).

After examining the text, we can see that Cornelius and those with him still needed baptism even though they had received the manifestation of the Holy Spirit. This points out that baptism is essential in order to be redeemed through Christ.

A3 CORNELIUS RECEIVING THE SPIRIT PRIOR TO BAPTISM

1. Gareth L. Reese, pages 410 and 411.
2. G.R. Beasley-Murray, page 108.
3. Ibid, page 108.
4. Reese, page 411.

A4 INFANT BAPTISM AND ORIGINAL SIN

Infant baptism is practiced by several groups and is tied to the concept of original sin. Original sin is the concept that all mankind has been judged guilty along with Adam and we are born already a condemned sinner. Thus, we are condemned before we committed a sin of our own.

Mattox says in his book *The Eternal Kingdom,* "The doctrine of original sin teaches that children are born with the guilt of sin and through inheritance are depraved in nature. This idea is not found in any of the extant works of the Apostolic Fathers."[1] Mattox identifies the Apostolic Fathers as: "The uninspired writers who did their work from the year 100 to 150 are generally referred to as the Apostolic Fathers. These are men who knew the Apostles or knew people who had known them and had received their teaching in this direct manner."[2] Mattox tells us that:

> Tertullian (160-220) is the first to formulate the doctrine of original sin. He taught that the soul shares in Adam's guilt and every man therefore is under condemnation and is punishable for his inherited guilt quite apart from any actual sin he may commit. Cyprian, while bishop of Carthage (248-258) enlarged upon Tertullian's conception and declared that even though an infant had committed no actual sin it needed forgiveness for the sin inherited from Adam and this was received in baptism.[3]

Tertullian wrote during the second and third centuries after Christ. He had not had any direct contact with the apostles of Jesus nor with anyone else who had. Prior to his writings there is no indication of the doctrine of original sin being passed on to all mankind. Without that doctrine, infant baptism serves no purpose.

Beasley-Murray writes;

> The New Testament gives no evidence that infant baptism was practiced in the primitive Church; its theology of baptism is lofty, with no taint of magical conceptions, and does not allow of application to the baptism of infants.[4]

Remember Hebrews 8:7-13 where we are told those entering into the New Covenant do not need to be taught of God because they knew about God already before they are in the covenant relationship. Whereas under the Old or Mosaic Covenant, boys entered that covenant eight days after birth and then had to be taught. Without a commitment of the one being baptized, the act and the element of water do absolutely nothing.

Consider carefully what God's word says about inheriting sins. Israel had a proverb in the days of Ezekiel, *"The fathers eat the sour grapes, but the children's teeth are set on edge"* (Ezekiel 18:2b).

God told Ezekiel that they are not to use this proverb again (Ezekiel 18:3). God makes it clear that we do not inherit sin. "The person who sins will die. The son will not bear the punishment for the father's iniquity, nor will the father bear the punishment for the son's iniquity; the righteousness of the righteous will be upon himself, and the wickedness of the wicked will be upon himself" (Ezekiel 18:20). The fact that individuals are held responsible for only their own actions is borne out in II Kings 14:6 and Ezekiel 18:4.

Since we do not inherit our father's sins, it makes sense that we are also not born with Adam's sin laid on us. We will not be held accountable for anyone else, but only for what we do. We inherited one of the consequences of Adam having sinned, which is physical death, but not his guilt. *"For as by a man came death, by a man has come also the resurrection of the dead. For as in Adam all die, so also in Christ shall all be made alive"* (I Corinthians 15:21-22 ESV). Our personal sin puts each one of us under sentence of spiritual death or separation from God. This is not because Adam's having sinned automatically makes us sinners, but because we have sinned.

Therefore, we are not born sinners because we have Adam's sin put upon us. We enter life sinless and stay that way until we personally sin.

The question is "How does God deal with infants, children, and mentally diminished people?" I knew when I needed a Savior, and that without Jesus I was lost and helpless to make anything right. I clearly understood that God would hold me accountable. As I read God's word, I can see that it is understandable to me. However, can an infant understand even if you read the Bible to him? In the same way, can a person with severely mentally diminished reasoning understand?

We need to look at this issue beginning with God's characteristics or nature. We have a tendency to think of God by single characteristics, which then causes us to have a simplistic view of God. For example, if God is only love, then we don't have to do anything. We will be forgiven without even repenting. Conversely, if God is wrathful only, then there is no hope. God cannot and should not be put in a box. God's nature or characteristics include love, holiness, righteousness, sinlessness, patience, justice, honesty, wrath, and completely trustworthiness. What His characteristics mean is that a totally just God will not condemn anyone who is not capable of understanding right from wrong or good from evil.

A believer having the idea of original sin may quote, "For as through the one man's disobedience the many were made sinners" (Romans 5:19a). It appears that Paul is saying that because Adam sinned by disobeying God's command, we are automatically judged as having sinned by God.

Let us go back to the beginning. In Genesis 2:17 the penalty for eating of the tree of the knowledge of good and evil is death. Adam and Eve disobeyed and ate of that tree. God pronounced curses (Genesis 3:9-19). They died that very day by being separated from God's presence. They no longer walked and talked with God daily. The next thing that we read is, *"Then the Lord God said, 'Behold, the man has become like one of Us, knowing good and evil; and now, he might stretch out his hand, and take also from the tree of life, and eat, and live forever — therefore the Lord God sent him out from the garden of Eden"* (Genesis 3:22-23a).

The penalty of death has two parts. The first is separation from God, and the second is physical death. As someone said, "The minute we are born we begin to die." Definitely, we have inherited as a result of Adam's sin physical death. Romans 5:19 goes on to say, *"Even so through the obedience of the One the many will be made righteous."* When we are in Christ, we are made righteous. The question is how do we understand the word *made*? Vine says that it is a strong word signifying "to appoint a person to a position."[5]

Like Adam, we all have sinned. *"Therefore, just as through one man sin entered into the world, and death through sin, and so death spread to all men, because all sinned"* (Romans 5:12). If we are viewed and treated by God as sinners because we are guilty of Adam's sin, then the scriptures such as Ezekiel 18 above are contradicted. We cannot have Adam's sin dumped on us and at the same time not be held accountable for our father's sins.

Strong puts it this way, "The Scripture, on the contrary, declares that Adam's offense *constituted* us sinners (Rom. 5:19). We are not sinners simply because God regards and treats us as such, but God regards us as sinners because we are sinners."[6]

A righteous and just God cannot be true to His nature if He judges and condemns people because of what others have done or failed to do. I also believe that a just God will not condemn anyone who is incapable of understanding right and wrong.

David wrote, *"O Lord, You have searched me and known me....You understand my thought from afar....Even before there is a word on my tongue, behold, O Lord, You know it all"* (Psalm 139:1-4). *"I, the Lord, search the heart, I test the mind, even to give to each man according to his ways, according to the results of his deeds"* (Jeremiah 17:10). *"God is a righteous judge"* (Psalm 7:11a). Above all, God is an impartial judge (Acts 10:34-35).

We cannot ask for a fairer judge to stand before. He knows our motives, our reasons, and our emotions; therefore, His judgments are just and fair. God deals with us on the basis of our believing or not believing in Him, and our obedience to Him (II Thessalonians 1:8).

A4 INFANT BAPTISM AND ORIGINAL SIN

1. F.W. Mattox, *The Eternal Kingdom,* page 117.
2. Ibid, pages 55-56.
3. Ibid, page 117.
4. G.R. Beasley-Murray, page 358.
5. *Vine's Expository Dictionary of Biblical Words, A Complete Expository Dictionary of the Old And New Testaments in One Volume,* Editors: W.E. Vine, Merrill F. Unger, and William White, jr., Thomas Nelson Publishers, Nashville, Camden, New York, 1985. Page 50 of An Expository Dictionary of New Testament Words with their Precise Meanings for English Readers, page 33.
6. Augustus Hopkins Strong, *Systematic Theology,* page 614.

A5 ME IN CHRIST VERSUS CHRIST IN ME

A favorite verse that has been used for connecting an unbeliever with Christ is, "Behold, I stand at the door and knock; if anyone hears My voice and opens the door, I will come in to him and will dine with him, and he with Me" (Revelation 3:20). It is important to understand the context in order to get the main meaning. It is said by Jesus to His church at Laodicea. They were lukewarm toward Him, and He warns that unless they repent, He will spit them out (Revelation 3:14-22). Jesus is asking believers who have not completely seated Him on the throne of their hearts to allow Him to have total authority over them. He is clearly not number one in their lives individually and collectively. He is standing outside His church and asking to be let in. Likewise, Jesus stands outside the door of our individual hearts and asks that we open and allow Him to truly be our Lord and God. Christ Jesus will not enter our hearts forcefully. He will only enter when we invite Him in and submit to His will.

Wayne Jackson in his commentary on Revelation writes, "The Laodicean congregation was lukewarm (3:16) – a condition that makes Christ sick. Their apathy was such that they had excluded the Son of God from their fellowship and he pled for reentry (3:20)."[1]

"But if Christ is in you, your body is dead because of sin, yet your spirit is alive because of righteousness" (Romans 8:10 NIV).

BAPTISM WHAT IS IT GOOD FOR?

Dan R. Owen says, "The one who is "in Christ" has Christ in him (Col. 1:27)."[2] Simply said, you cannot be in Christ without Him being in you. There is that very real close connection and relationship. The phrase in Romans 8:10 *"Though the body is dead because of sin"* means that our bodies are no longer controlled by our selfish nature. *"Even so consider yourselves to be dead to sin"* (Romans 6:11a).

We either turn our lives fully over to Christ's total control, or we try to share control. What we must learn is that either He fully controls us, or He is not on the throne of our lives.

"I have been crucified with Christ; and it is no longer I who live, but Christ lives in me; and the life which I now live in the flesh I live by faith in the Son of God, who loved me and gave Himself up for me" (Galatians 2:20). Robert L. Johnson comments on Galatians 2:20:

> For Christ, the cross was a complete break with this life. It was a radical change in relationship to all things — and so with Paul. The things that had mattered in his past life — hopes, ideals, ambitions, zeal for the law — these things were now dead for him. And Paul knew something about Christ's death. He had gone over to Christ's side. He took his stand with Christ even in his shame,[3]

Johnson continues, "But Paul's crucifixion with Christ had another side. It enabled him to live. **It is no longer I who live, but Christ who lives in me.** Paul is clearly speaking of spiritual fellowship with Christ."[4] Paul turned his life over to Jesus, totally allowing Jesus to use him to achieve God's purpose. Reading Paul's writings, we see that he had no regrets in spite of all he suffered. Frederic Rendall writes:

> As the resurrection of Christ was the sequel of the crucifixion, so Paul was joined to Christ in death that he might be joined to Him in spiritual life.... The new life is no longer, like the former, dependent on the struggling efforts of a mere man to draw near to God in his own righteousness. Christ Himself is its source, as the vine is the source of life to the branches.[5]

Paul is speaking of a new relationship. *"What is more, I consider everything a loss compared to the surpassing greatness of knowing Christ Jesus my Lord, for whose sake I have lost all things. I consider them rubbish, that I may gain Christ and be found in him, not having a righteousness of my own that comes from the law, but that which is through faith in Christ — the righteousness that comes from God and is by faith"* (Philippians 2:8-9 NIV).

For Paul, all his past accomplishments and standing among his peers was nothing compared to knowing Christ Jesus and having Him as Lord over his life. Christ Jesus should be number one in our lives. Our righteousness is from God, freely given us because of faith. Our faith is in Christ's gifting us with righteousness because of His sinless life and sacrifice. Like Paul, we need to have faith and trust in God's promises.

BAPTISM WHAT IS IT GOOD FOR?

Paul said, *"Follow my example, as I follow the example of Christ"* (I Corinthians 11:1 NIV). Paul considered unity with Jesus of utmost importance. *"I have been crucified with Christ and I no longer live, but Christ lives in me..."* (Galatians 2:20a). Because Christ Jesus gave His life for Paul, he now gives to Christ his life to rule and use. In Ephesians 3:14-19 Paul prays for the Ephesians and all followers of Jesus to allow Christ to dwell in them through faith. This is a new relationship, an intimate one with God through Christ Jesus. It is a united relationship which is manifested through our surrender to the will of God. The concept of Christ in us is a relational one. It is a willing submission to His will, His authority, and His rule over each one of us. The fact that Christ is in us and we are in Him clearly portrays an intimate relationship.

What about me being in Christ? *"For you died, and your life is now hidden with Christ in God"* (Colossians 3:3 NIV). Therefore, as Christ is in me, I am in Him. Paul said it this way, *"For all of you who were baptized into Christ have clothed yourselves with Christ"* (Galatians 3:27).

Hendriksen says:

> The apostle is speaking, therefore, not about the merely outward administration of baptism, as if some magical healing power is adhered to it, but about *the sign and seal in conjunction with that which is signified and sealed.* All those, then, who by means of their baptism have truly laid aside, in principle, their garment of sin, and have been

decked with the robe of Christ's righteousness, having thus been buried with him and raised with him have put on Christ (cf. Rom. 6:3ff.; 13:14; Col. 2:12, 13).[6]

Beasley-Murray comments:

> The old man is stripped off and the new man is put on, 'which is renewed in knowledge after the image of its creator. ... Here there cannot be Greek or Jew ... but Christ is all and in all'. The putting on the new man represents not a determination to turn over a new leaf and be a better man but the beginning of a new existence 'renewed after the image of God', *which image is Christ,* who is 'all, and in all'.[7]

When we are in Christ, God sees us as righteous. However, never forget that righteousness is not based on our earning it by living a sinless life; it is given to us by grace. It is the free gift of God. Being clothed in Christ is extremely important. Jesus taught in Matthew 22:1-14 that the attendee at the wedding banquet not dressed in the right clothes was thrown out. One can profess a belief in Christ Jesus, but unless he is clothed in Jesus, he is not properly dressed.

Hendriksen continues, "In Christ they have risen to newness of life. They have become united with him in the sense that he is the Life of their life, the Light of their light, the Strength of their strength."[8] Jesus is all we need and only in Him does life have any purpose and meaning.

"It is because of him that you are in Christ Jesus, who has become for us wisdom from God — that is, our righteousness, holiness, and redemption" (I Corinthians 1:30 NIV). *"He made Him who knew no sin to be sin on our behalf, so that we might become the righteousness of God in Him"* (II Corinthians 5:21).

Andrew Murray writes:

> The believers at Corinth were still feeble and carnal, only babes in Christ. And yet Paul wants them, at the outset of his preaching, to know distinctly that they are in Christ Jesus. The whole Christian life depends on the clear consciousness of our position in Christ. ... He (Paul) would have us not only remember our union to Christ, but specially that it is not our own doing, but the work of God Himself. [9]

Those who have been immersed and raised up are now clothed in Christ's righteousness and through continually studying His words and example are uniting with Him in purpose and in a changed attitude. The obedient believer lives in and for Christ Jesus knowing that real life and eternal salvation is found in Him alone.

Coffman in his commentary says:

> In Christ alone is there salvation; and in Christ the saved possess all things. Behold here the only true ground of justification in the eyes of God. Jesus is the perfect, holy, undefiled, righteous in the superlative degree. In Christ and as Christ and as fully identified with him, it is true also that Christians are holy, righteous, etc. It is not their righteousness, of course, in the sense that they achieved it [10]

A benefit of being in Jesus is that we now are righteous and holy before our heavenly Father. We are redeemed because Jesus took our sins upon Himself and gave us His righteousness. To receive these blessings of redemption, righteousness, and holiness we must be in Christ, that is, united with Him.

"You are all sons of God though faith in Christ Jesus, for all of you who were baptized into Christ have clothed yourselves with Christ" (Galatians 3:26-27 NIV).

Coffman says:

> It is not fair to leave this brief discussion of the salvation (inclusive of all spiritual blessings) which is *"in Christ,"* without pointing out for those who truly desire to know the truth that in all the holy scriptures there is no other way revealed by which a believer might acquire the status of being *"in*

Christ," except through being baptized *"into him"* (Rom. 6:3; Gal. 3:27; I Cor. 12:13).[11]

If we have died and been raised to the new life (Romans 6:3-4), then our lives have a new focus in Christ. Our thoughts should become like more of our Lord and our God.

> *Since, then, you have been raised with Christ, set your hearts on things above, where Christ is seated at the right hand of God. Set your minds on things above, not on earthly things. For you died, and your life is now hidden with Christ in God. When Christ, who is your life, appears, then you also will appear with him in glory (Colossians 3:1-4 NIV).*

We are ever striving to mature in Christ so that when people see us, they see Jesus instead of us.

A5 ME IN CHRIST VERSUS CHRIST IN ME

1. Wayne Jackson, *Revelation: Jesus Christ's Final Message of Hope, Selected Studies from The Apocalypse,* Christian Courier Publications, Inc., 7809 N. Pershing Avenue, Stockton, CA 95207, 2004, page 36.
2. Dan R. Owen, *The Righteousness of God Study Notes on Romans,* Bear Valley School of Biblical Studies, Denver, Colorado, 1984, page 53.
3. Robert L. Johnson, *The Letter of Paul to The Galatians,* The Living Word Commentary, R,B, Sweet Co., Inc., Austin, Texas, 1969, page 71.
4. Ibid, page 72.
5. Frederic Randall, *The Epistle To The Galatians,* The Expositor's Greek Testament, Volume III, Edited by, W. Robertson Nicoll, Wm. B. Eerdmans Publishing Company, Grand Rapids, Michigan, reprinted 1974, page 166.
6. William Hendriksen, *Exposition of Galatians, Ephesians, Philippians, Colossians, and Philemon,* page 149.
7. G. R. Beasley-Murray, *Baptism in the New Testament,* page 149.
8. Hendriksen, page 149.
9. Andrew Murray, *Abide in Christ,* Barbour and Company, Inc., Uhrichsville, Ohio, 1992, page 39.

10. James Burton Coffman, *Commentary on 1 and 2 Corinthians,* page 24.
11. Ibid, page 25.

A6 BAPTISM FOR THE DEAD

"Now if there is no resurrection, what will those do who are baptized for the dead? If the dead are not raised at all, why are people baptized for them?" (I Corinthians 15:29 NIV)

I Corinthians 15:29 opens up a whole new can of worms.

Baptism for the dead. Also known as "baptism by proxy" or "vicarious baptism," this Ordinance is performed in Mormon temples by living church members on behalf of someone who is deceased. The soul for whom the work is done is given a chance to receive the gospel in Spirit Prison, though acceptance by the deceased person is not guaranteed. According to Joseph Smith, "The greatest responsibility in this world that God has placed upon us is to seek after our dead" (Teachings of the Prophet Joseph Smith, p. 356). Tenth President Joseph Fielding Smith explained, "Since the requirement of obedience to the Gospel ordinances is made of all men, and since they cannot enter into the kingdom without complying with the law the Lord has given, a work must be done in behalf of those who have died without knowledge of the Gospel and its requirements, and who never had the opportunity of repentance and remission of

sins" (The Way to Perfection, p. 152). And fifteenth President Gordon B. Hinckley stated, "Through living proxies who stand in behalf of the dead, the same ordinances are available to those who have passed from mortality. In the spirit world they then are free to accept or reject those earthly ordinances performed for them, including baptism, marriage, and the sealing of family relationships. There must be no compulsion in the work of the Lord, but there must be opportunity"1

This view of "baptism by proxy" is at odds with what the Scriptures teach. We learn that salvation is personal. In all accounts of non-Christians being baptized in the Scriptures, there is no example of Christians being baptized for dead people in the Bible. There is certainly no example of having a stand-in who is baptized for another.

There are some who believe that the living faithful can be baptized for those who have died outside of Christ. This concept negates the teaching of God that says we are individually responsible. As pointed out in this book, Ezekiel 18 makes it clear that we are responsible for how we use our lives. I will not be held accountable for my father's sins and I will not be righteous because of my father's righteousness. Listen to God. *"No man can by any means redeem his brother or give to God a ransom for him — for the redemption of his soul is costly"* (Psalm 49:7-8a). This idea that I can be redeemed after death, or I can repent after I die is contrary to the Scriptures, *"And just as it is appointed for man to die once, and after that comes the judgment"* (Hebrews 9:27 ESV).

Jesus made it clear in the example of Lazarus and the rich man (Luke 16:19-31). Jesus says that after death our state is fixed. "And besides all this, between us and you a chasm has been fixed, in order that those who would pass from here to you may not be able, and none may cross from there to us" (Luke 19:26 ESV).

Luke 16:19-31 shows that after death we are either in comfort or torment. However, some scholars interpret Luke 16:19-31 as a parable and thus make it a story teaching take care of those in need. Bernard Ramm says this about parables, "A parable is some commonly known earthly thing … It is this concrete and pictorial grounding which make them such remarkable instruments for instruction. … This earthly element bears an analogical relationship which gives the parable its illustrative, or argumentative force."[2] We do not see any earthly element in these verses. Honestly, if Jesus used Lazarus and the rich man as a warning to the Pharisees to frighten them with no real truth behind His words, then He is deliberately misleading them and us. It is like a frustrated parent saying to a child, "You do that one more time and I'll kill you." The child knows that won't happen. We must understand that Jesus in His ministry discussed hell and torment after death at least twenty-five times.

BAPTISM WHAT IS IT GOOD FOR?

Jesus went to the cross freely to stand in our place and save us from God's wrath. Think about all that Jesus suffered, leaving heaven and His glory, being born, growing up, being tempted, being arrested, and being tortured, and killed in order to redeem us. Eternal punishment is real; otherwise, there would be no need for the cross.

"Now if there is no resurrection, what will those do who are baptized for the dead? If the dead are not raised at all, why are people baptized for them?" (I Corinthians 15:29 NIV)

Okay, so what does I Corinthians 15:29 mean?

> Looking back in this section we see a problem in the church at Corinth which Paul had to deal with. "Now if Christ is proclaimed as raised from the dead, how can some of you say that there is no resurrection of the dead? But if there is no resurrection of the dead, then not even Christ has been raised" (I Corinthians 15:12-13 ESV). There were some within the church denying a resurrection. *"But in fact Christ has been raised from the dead, the firstfruits of those who have fallen asleep"* (I Corinthians 15:20 ESV). The resurrection of Jesus proves that He is the Promised Anointed One of God. Peter said in the first gospel message, *"God has made Him both Lord and Christ — this Jesus whom you crucified"* (Acts 2:36b).

A dilemma of those who argue that the dead are only those who never had a chance to hear the Gospel must face is that the references to the dead are generally believers, as opposed to unbelievers. In I Corinthians 15:12 the dead could also include even those being raised to be cast away from God. The use of "fallen asleep" (I Corinthians 15:18) helps us to understand that the physically dead, not the spiritual, are under discussion.

The Greek word translated for in the original can also be understood as *"on behalf of"*. This could be understood as following the example of others who have been baptized.

Some say Paul was making an argument based on a practice of those who being baptized for family or friends who had died. While Coffman mentions this explanation, he also tells us that there is no historical evidence for it.[3]

As to Paul approving the validity of baptizing a dead unbeliever, Coffman comments;

> Paul here used an argumentum ad hominem, that is, an argument based upon what men were doing, indicating clearly enough that some persons known to the Corinthians were practicing a baptism for the benefit of the dead; but the one thing that makes it impossible to suppose Paul approved of such a thing is the use of the third person pronouns. There are no examples in the NT practice of Christians being designated as what "they" do. Concerning Christian baptism, for example, it is always "we" or "you" who were baptized and addressed in the

first or second persons, never in the third person. It is still "they" not "we" who baptize for the dead!"[4]

While we may grapple with what exactly is said and meant by "baptized for the dead," we must accept that God's word clearly teaches individual responsibility. The Scriptures make it plain when we die, we will face judgment (Hebrews 9:27). Jesus explained when we die, we will either be in comfort or torment (Luke 16:19-31). The great chasm between the states of comfort and torment shows that the fate of those who have physically died is irreversible (Luke 16:26). There are no second chances after death.

A6 BAPTISM FOR THE DEAD

1. (*Be Thou an Example*, p. 131).[1] https://www.mrm.org/ Mormonism Research Ministry *Baptism for the Dead Definition.*
2. Bernard Ramm, *Protestant Biblical Interpretation,* Third Revised Edition, Baker Books, A Division of Baker Book House, Grand Rapids, Michigan 49516, 2005, pages 278 and 279.
3. James Burton Coffman, *Commentary on 1 and 2 Corinthians,* page 260.
4. Ibid, page 260.

This Special Study, "Baptism for the Dead," is based upon a paper titled *Baptism For The Dead* written by Rob Redden, minister of the Church of Christ in Grover Beach, California. I am indebted to him for his gracious permission to use his paper and research in my study.

A7 IS IT POSSIBLE TO FALL FROM GRACE?

Jesus said, *"Not everyone who says to Me, 'Lord, Lord,' will enter the kingdom of heaven, but who does the will of My Father who is in heaven will enter. Many will say to Me on that day, 'Lord, Lord, did we not prophesy in Your name, and in Your name cast out demons, and in Your name perform many miracles?' And then I will declare to them, 'I never knew you; depart from Me, you who practice lawlessness'"* (Matthew 7:21-23). Jesus excludes people who did great deeds in His name, but who failed to do the Father's will. Those people are not allowed into the kingdom of heaven. A person must submit to the will of the Father to be saved, even by grace.

The Spirit through the writer of Hebrews gives us an example to consider. The Israelites who were led out of Egypt by Moses died in the wilderness. They were not allowed to enter the Promised Land, which is referred to as God's rest. There are two reasons. *"And to whom did He swear that they would not enter His rest, but to those who were disobedient? So, we see that they were not able to enter because of unbelief"* (Hebrews 3:18-19). God gives two reasons, which are disobedience and unbelief. The writer goes on to tell us that we can fail to enter God's rest, which is heaven, *"Therefore, let us fear if, while a promise remains of entering His rest, any one of you may seem to have come short of it"* (Hebrews 4:1). Note that the Israelites were in a covenant relationship with God (Exodus chapters 19-24). In spite of having witnessed

God's power, His grace toward them, and His caring for them in the wilderness wandering, they proved to be disobedient and unbelieving.

The fact that those that were brought out of Egyptian bondage by Moses were God's people, the redeemed, cannot be denied. Paul used them as an example to the Corinthians and us as well. Consider carefully:

> *For I do want you to be unaware, brothers, that our fathers were all under the cloud, and all passed through the sea, and all were baptized into Moses in the cloud and in the sea, and all ate the same spiritual food, and all drank the same spiritual drink. For they drank from the spiritual Rock that followed them, and the Rock was Christ.* (I Corinthians 10:1-4 ESV).

At Mount Sinai the people were asked to commit to obeying God. *"Moses came and told the people all; the words of the Lord and all the rules. And all the people answered with one voice and said, 'All the words that the Lord has spoken we will do'"* (Exodus 24:3 ESV).

> *Then he took the Book of the Covenant and read it in the hearing of the people. And they said, 'All that the Lord has spoken we will do, and we will be obedient,' And Moses took the blood of the covenant and threw it on the people and said, 'Behold the blood of the covenant that the Lord has made with you in accordance with all these words'* (Exodus 24:7-8 ESV).

BAPTISM WHAT IS IT GOOD FOR?

For whom were those who heard and yet rebelled? Was it not all those who left Egypt led by Moses? And with whom was he provoked for forty years? Was it not with those who sinned, whose bodies fell in the wilderness? And to whom did he swear that they would not enter his rest, but to those who were disobedient? So we see that they were unable to enter because of unbelief. (Hebrews 3:16-19 ESV).

Paul tells us, *"Now these things took place as examples for us, that we might not desire evil as they did"* (I Corinthians 10:6 ESV). The Hebrews writer said, *"Take care brothers, lest there be in any of you an evil, unbelieving heart leading you to fall away from the living God"* (Hebrews 3:12 ESV). These events recorded in God's word should serve as a warning to us to take heed as to how we stand so that we too do not sin and turn from Christ. If these-covenant related people could be rejected, what makes us think that God is different today?

God's grace can be rejected by covenant-related people through disobedience, unbelief, and not doing the heavenly Father's will. *"For if, after they have escaped the defilements of the world by the knowledge of the Lord and Savior Jesus Christ, they are again entangled in them and are overcome, the last state has become worse for them than the first. For it would be better for them not to have known the way of righteousness, than having known it, to turn away from the holy commandment handed on to them. It has happened to them according to the true proverb, 'A dog returns to its own vomit,' 'A sow, after washing, returns to wallowing in the mire"* (II Peter 2:20-22).

Were these people who had turned away from the holy commandment really Christians or just people pretending to follow Jesus? Consider the language in II Peter 1:4, *"For by these He has granted to us His precious and magnificent promises, so that by them you may become partakers of the divine nature, having escaped the corruption that is in the world by lust."*

It is through God's great promise of forgiveness and redemption anchored firmly in the sacrificial offering of His only begotten Son, Jesus, that we escape corruption. Those to whom Peter is writing in chapter one, verse four and chapter two, verse twenty all have escaped the world. No one escapes from the corruption and defilements of the world without committing to and being united with Christ Jesus. Therefore, clearly, they had been true Christians, and for whatever reason, they turned back to the world and left Jesus.

Bruce Oberst writes, "The persons described had been Christians. They had fled from and were free from the world's defilements."[1]

William Barclay says, "(IV) He is the *Christ by whom we escape the world's corruption.*"[2]

Barclay goes on to say, "If they had once known the real way of Christ and have relapsed into this their case is even worse."[3]

BAPTISM WHAT IS IT GOOD FOR?

N.T. Caton agrees.

> By being taught of God, and learning thereby what we must do to become his children, which includes a knowledge of the Lord Jesus Christ; in short, having put on Christ, become his subjects, and, by the means so graciously provided for us by a loving Father, having escaped from the world and all its pollutions. Now, in case we become entangled in them again with the allurements of the world, and are thus overcome and apostatized, what of our condition then? This last state is worse for us than the state from which we escaped at our conversion to Christ.[4]

Note that the Spirit through Peter says that when those who have escaped from the world by learning about Jesus the Lord and Savior and are again joined with the world, their situation is now worse than it was before. The only way that I know to escape the defilements of the world is to be in Christ. You cannot escape from being a sinner by simply knowing about Christ. You are still in the first condition as a slave to sin. II Peter 2:20-22 ties in with what is said in Hebrews.

"For if we go on sinning willfully after receiving the knowledge of the truth, there no longer remains a sacrifice for sins...How much severer punishment do you think that he will deserve who has trampled underfoot the Son of God, and has regarded as unclean the blood of the covenant by which he was sanctified, and has insulted the

Spirit of grace?" (Hebrews 10:26-29) The person here was sanctified and then rejected Jesus the gift of God. You cannot get any plainer statement than that. That person was saved and still continued to live a life dedicated to sin.

Edward Fudge in commenting on Hebrews 10:26 wrote:

> To **sin willfully** is not to commit a single sinful act of weakness or ignorance, but, as the Greek verb form indicates, to continue in a constant practice of sin. Nor is **sin** here just any kind of sin, but specifically the sin of disbelief which shows itself in forsaking Christ altogether.[5]

The Scripture plainly states that the one deserving of a severer punishment was sanctified by the shed blood of Christ. That person had received the knowledge of the truth and was forgiven of his sins, thanks to Jesus' sacrifice on the cross. He then turns back to a life of willfully sinning; therefore, his punishment promises to be very severe. The idea is that God has picked out the perfect gift, salvation, at the price of sacrificing of His only begotten Son, and that gift is not appreciated at all.

Disbelief can be manifested by not trusting that Jesus paid our debt of sin totally. It is like saying that the good works that we do count toward earning ten percent of getting to be in heaven, and grace through Jesus covers the remaining ninety percent. Jesus's sacrifice covers us one hundred percent. What we do has nothing whatsoever to do with earning salvation. Our works are proof that we are doing the Father's will and are being transformed.

BAPTISM WHAT IS IT GOOD FOR?

The point is that while grace is free and available universally, there are some who will not accept it, and there are even those, who having accepted grace, choose to walk away.

You say, "But God will never stop loving us," and quote, Romans 8:31-39. I agree with you that there is no circumstance, no one, and nothing in all creation that can separate us from the love of God. However, I can let go of God's hand, I can choose to continue being the center of my universe, and I can decide to regard Christ's sacrifice as being valueless. I can decide that God's love just isn't worth it even after I've accepted it.

Paul said, *"I do not nullify the grace of God, for if righteousness comes through the Law, then Christ died needlessly"* (Galatians 2:21). In other words, if we can earn righteousness by law keeping or even by good works, then there is no point for God's grace and Christ's atoning death. We cannot earn a righteous or a forgiven state before God because there is nothing that we can do or offer to negate the penalty for sin. As James wrote, *"For whoever keeps the whole law and yet stumbles in one point, he has become guilty of all"* (James 2:10). We must understand that if we try to be good enough and live and think like God requires, we must not be lawbreakers in even one small point. That goes back to the point that we became accountable for our actions and thoughts until the day we die.

We see in Galatians 5:4, *"You have been severed from Christ, you are seeking to be justified by law; you have fallen from grace."*

Consider what Cecil May, Jr., comments about falling from grace:

> People who believe "once saved, always saved" generally believe one who prays for forgiveness and invites Jesus into one's heart is forever saved, regardless of the life lived. Some, at least, say one who lives a blatantly sinful life was never saved in the first place. While that is true of some, it is not true of all. The Bible tells of some who have "fallen away from grace" (Galatians 5:4). You cannot fall away from where you have not been.[6]

You cannot be severed from something that you were not part of in the first place. However, does this mean that every time a Christian sins he falls out of grace and is lost until he repents and asks for forgiveness? That would a horrible life and would negate what John wrote, *"I write these things to you who believe in the name of the Son of God so that you may know that you have eternal life"* (I John 5:13).

Our walking in faith means we trust in God's grace. We also understand that our minds need to be focused on spiritual things (Romans 8:1-11). Therefore, when the Christian is walking in the light, the blood of Jesus continuously cleanses him from all sin (I John 1:7). A Christian is capable of sinning, but if he is walking in the light, he has a repentant heart, so he is confident in his salvation knowing God will forgive. Now a Christian that takes grace for granted will ignore his sins and not feel real sorrow and definitely not ask for forgiveness. When we sin and since we are walking in the light, we will experience sorrow which causes us to ask for forgiveness knowing that our Father is willing to forgive us (I John 1:8).

We can choose to sin and walk in darkness after we were saved and had the Spirit within us. There comes a time when God will remove the Holy Spirit from within us. *"Now the Spirit of the Lord departed from Saul"* (I Samuel 16:14a). Saul had been God's first anointed king of Israel, and because Saul disobeyed, God removed His Spirit from him. Therefore, Saul was no longer connected with God. In Ezekiel chapter Ten the prophet tells of God departing from the Holy of Holies in the temple because of the continual sins of the nation. God said in the days of Noah, *"My Spirit shall not strive with man forever"* (Genesis 6:3b).

The Spirit in Hebrews says, *"If we deliberately keep on sinning after we have received the knowledge of the truth, no sacrifice for sins is left, but only a fearful expectation of judgement and of raging fire that will consume the enemies of God"* (Hebrews 10:26-27 NIV). Then, *"How much more severely do you think a man deserves to be punished who has trampled the Son of God under foot, who has treated as an unholy thing the blood of the covenant that sanctified him, and who has insulted the Spirit of grace?"* (Hebrews 10:29 NIV). It is very plain the one being discussed here was washed by the blood and sanctified. Jesus said to His church in Laodicea that because they didn't care, He was ready to spit them out. Yet, He called for them to wake up and repent (Revelation 3:14-19 NIV).

A7 IS IT POSSIBLE TO FALL FROM GRACE?

1. Bruce Oberst, *Letters from Peter,* Bible Study Textbook Series, College Press. Joplin, Missouri, April 1979, page 180.
2. William Barclay, *The Letters of James and Peter,* page 297.
3. Ibid, page 335.
4. N. T. Caton, *A Commentary and an Exposition of the Epistles of James, Peter, John, and Jude,* page 130.
5. Edward Fudge, *Our Man in Heaven an Exposition of the Epistle to the Hebrews,* page 114.
6. Cecil May, Jr., *Bible Questions & Answers,* "The Magnolia Messenger", Volume 42 – Number 2, Summer 2020, page 13.

A8 WHAT DO THE WORDS *WATER AND THE SPIRIT* IN JOHN 3:5 MEAN?

"Jesus answered him. "Truly, truly, I say to you. Unless one is born again, he cannot see the kingdom of God" (John 3:3 ESV).

"Truly, truly, I say to you, unless one is born of water and the Spirit, he cannot enter the kingdom of heaven (John 3:5 ESV).

The problem that we face is what is meant by "water and the Spirit?" Does *water* refer to physical birth or spirit or baptism? What does *the Spirit* exactly mean? To clarify these issues, we need to examine *born again,* for there are translations that translate the original word for *again* with the phrase *born from above.*

Beasley-Murray writes:

> Calvin considered that water and Spirit mean the same thing, "for it as a frequent and common way of speaking in Scripture, when the Spirit is mentioned, to add the word *Water* or *Fire*, expressing his power, in support of which Mt. 3:11, Lk. 3:16 are quoted. But in the latter two passages it is unlikely that 'fire' is a symbol for the Holy Spirit; it represents a quite a different notion of judgement. Calvin's exegesis was forced on him because he could not endure the idea that baptism was necessary to salvation ('Commentary on St. John's Gospel', vol. I, *E. T.,* 1846, p.110).[1]

BAPTISM WHAT IS IT GOOD FOR?

Marcus Dods says regarding Calvin, "The two names cover one reality. ... And he defends this by a reference to the Baptist's announcement that the Messiah would baptize with the spirit and fire."[2]

This idea of identifying the Spirit with water also comes from what Jesus said, *"Jesus stood up and cried out. 'If anyone thirsts, let him come to me and drink. Whoever believes in me, as the Scripture has said,' 'Out of his heart will flow rivers of living water."* Now this he said about the Spirit" (John 7:37b-39a ESV).

Because of this some would have Jesus saying, "Unless one is born of spirit and the Spirit." Others have said that unless one is physically born and then born of the Spirit, they will not see the kingdom of heaven. Logically, this later idea is an absurdity because if one has not entered into this life through birth, one certainly cannot be born of the Spirit. Another question raised is are there two rebirths? One rebirth being born again of water and another born again of the Spirit.

There is the question of the meaning of the word translated "again." "*Anōthen* signifies 'from above, or anew.'"[3] M. R. Vincent says:

> In favor of the other rendering, *again,* it may be said: (1) that from above does not describe the fact but the nature of the new birth, which in the logical order would be stated after the fact, but which is first announced if we render *from above*. If we translate *anew* or *again,* the logical order is

preserved, the nature of the birth being described in ver. 5. (2) That Nicodemus clearly understood the word as meaning *again,* since, in ver. 4, he translated it into a *second time.*[4]

The context of the discussion between Jesus and Nicodemus requires that the translators translate the original as *born again, anew,* or *born a second time.* Since Jesus did not correct Nicodemus' response of being born again coming out of his mother a second time. This is what He meant. Jesus then corrected Nicodemus as He explained the second birth involved two elements, water and the Spirit.

Paul wrote:

> *But when the goodness and loving kindness of God our Savior appeared, he saved us, not because of works done by us in righteousness, but according to his own mercy,* **by the washing of regeneration and the renewal of the Holy Spirit,** *whom he poured out on us richly through Jesus Christ our Savior* (Titus 3:4-6 ESV). (Bold mine)

We have salvation only because God has given it to us. No matter how good our works are, we cannot do enough to earn salvation. Salvation is from God's mercy and accomplished by the washing of regeneration; that is our being given a new life (Romans 6:4). Our renewal is of the Holy Spirit. God richly poured out the Spirit on us through Jesus.

BAPTISM WHAT IS IT GOOD FOR?

Paul said, *"For we ourselves were once foolish, disobedient, led astray, slaves to various passions and pleasures, passing our days in malice and envy, hated by others and hating one another"* (Titus 3:3 ESV). Our sinful lives must be done away with and we need to have our lives regenerated. Our self-directed lives need to be restored to a God-directed life.

Speaking of our situation prior to being clothed in Christ, Paul gives us these identifying characteristics — helpless, ungodly, sinners, enemies, and subjects of God's wrath (Romans 5:6-10).

While God was speaking to Israel through His prophet Ezekiel, the words given shows God's consistency in a changing of lives from an ungodly nature to a renewed nature which is the nature that we were created to have.

> *Therefore, O house of Israel, I will judge you, each one according to his ways, declares the Sovereign Lord. Repent! Turn away from all your offenses, then sin will not be your downfall. Rid yourselves of all the offenses you have committed, and get a new heart and a new spirit. Why will you die, O house of Israel? For I take no pleasure in the death of anyone, declares the Sovereign Lord. Repent and live! (Ezekiel 18:30-32 NIV).*

Even though God will punish the entire nation of Israel, He judges each individual alone. The nation of Israel went into captivity because all within that nation sinned against God.

They are told to repent and turn their lives around. Then God will give them a new heart and a new spirit. In reference to a new heart and a new spirit, C. F. Kiel writes:

> A man cannot, indeed, create either of these by his own power; God alone can give them (ch. 11:19). But a man both can and should come to God to receive them: in other words, he can turn to God, and let both heart and spirit be renewed by the Spirit of God. And this God is willing to do.[5]

Along with Ezekiel 18:31 we read, "*I will give them an undivided heart and put a new spirit in them; I will move from them a heart of stone and give them a heart of flesh*" (Ezekiel 11:19 NIV). God gives us a new heart. It all gets back to grace.

Paul in telling the Jews what he was told by Ananias. "*And now what are you waiting for? Get up, be baptized and wash your sins away, calling his names.*" (Acts 22:16 NIC).

The idea of being born again signifies a new life. We recognize that as a clean slate with all our past sins washed away. The rebirth is pictured in the act of baptism or immersion.

> *Do you not know that all of us who have been baptized into Christ Jesus were baptized into his death? We were buried therefore with him by baptism into death, in order that, just as Christ was*

BAPTISM WHAT IS IT GOOD FOR?

> *raised from death by the glory of the Father, we too might walk in newness of life (Romans 6:3-4 ESV).*
>
> *Having been buried with him in baptism, in which you were also raised with him through faith in the powerful working of God, who raised him from the dead. And you, who were dead in your trespasses and the uncircumcision of your flesh, God mage alive together with him, having forgiven us all our trespasses, by canceling the record of debt that stood against us with its legal demands (Colossians 2:12-14 ESV).*

Prior to being born again we were spiritually dead, condemned by our sins. When because of our faith we are buried in the water of baptism, we are raised up just like Jesus was raised from the tomb by God the Father. Jesus now had a new glorified body, and we have a new cleansed life. The act of immersion pictures the rebirth beautifully.

The new birth is a result of God's grace. *"For it is by grace you have been saved, through faith — and this not from yourselves, it is the gift of God"* (Ephesians 2:8 NIV). God's grace centers on the sacrificial death of His only begotten Son, Jesus. *"God made him who had no sin to be sin for us, so that in him we might become the righteousness of God"* (II Corinthians 5:21 NIV).

Do not be surprised that to receive God's grace we must have faith in the effective sacrifice of Jesus. Faith in the fact that Jesus' sacrifice paid our debt completely, wiped it right off the books. Understand that there is no good deed, work, or anything that earns salvation. Jesus paid the full price that redeems us. To say that I must contribute to my salvation is to say that Jesus didn't pay the debt in full.

Being immersed in the watery grave of baptism pictures the fact that we are dead in our sins. We come to Jesus because we know that we are condemned and we want redemption. We are buried and freed from our sins and our self-directed nature. We are resurrected to a new clean life hidden in Christ.

Water plays an important part of the rebirth. The Spirit is the second part of the rebirth process.

We are given the Spirit at baptism. *"Peter replied, 'Repent and be baptized, every one of you, in the name of Jesus Christ for the forgiveness of your sins. And you will receive the gift of the Holy Spirit"* (Acts 2:38 NIV). Understand that the Holy Spirit is the gift given by God. Peter and the apostles before the Jewish high priest and Sanhedrin said; *"We are witnesses of these things, and so is the Holy Spirit, whom God has given to those who obey him"* (Acts 5:32 NIV).

Every person who has repented of his or her sins and been baptized has been given the Holy Spirit. The Lord who knows the heart of all is the one who adds the individual to the church. The Spirit is given only to those who sincerely believe, repent, and obey (Acts 2:47).

Peter and the apostles did not say, "the Holy Spirit, whom God has given all those who believe." They said, *"Whom*

BAPTISM WHAT IS IT GOOD FOR?

God has given to those who obey him." The Scriptures make it clear that all obedient believers are given the Holy Spirit.

We are no longer driven by the flesh, our worldly nature when we have been born again. Paul wrote; "You, however, are not in the flesh but in the Spirit, if in fact the Spirit of God dwells in you. Anyone who does not have the Spirit of Christ does not belong to him" (Romans 8:9 ESV).

"Do you not know that your body is a temple of the Holy Spirit, who is in you, whom you have received from God? You are not your own; you were bought at a price. Therefore honor God with your body" (I Corinthians 6:19-20 NIV). Having the Spirit within us is an encouragement to strive to live a godly life. We are told, *"And do not grieve the Holy Spirit of God, with whom you were sealed for the day of redemption"* (Ephesians 4:30 NIV). Do not continue to keep sinning believing that grace will always cover you.

Having the indwelling of the Spirit identifies those who have Him as Christians. *"The Spirit himself bears witness with our spirit that we are children of God"* (Romans 8:16 ESV). This function of the Holy Spirit reminds me of the Identification Friend or Foe system on military warplanes. They have transponders which enable a pilot to know if a plane is friend or foe. The indwelling Spirit marks those that He indwells as Christians.

Because those who have been baptized into Christ are now clothed with Jesus and are sons, they have been given the Spirit. The Spirit calls out "Abba, Father" signifying their sonship and affirming that they are heirs. (Romans 8:14-17, Galatians 3:26-4:7)

The Spirit helps us when we do not know what we should pray for because He knows our concerns and what is in our hearts (Romans 8:26-27).

The Holy Spirit also helps us develop His fruit. *"But the fruit of the Spirit is love, joy, peace, patience, kindness, goodness, faithfulness, gentleness, and self-control"* (Galatians 5:22-23 NIV). The Spirit is working on us when we are submissive and putting God's word in us, especially as we look at Jesus and desire to be more like our Lord.

When Jesus told Nicodemus that he needed to be born again of water and the Spirit, it is clear that He was referring to immersion in water and receiving the gift of the Holy Spirit. If there is no change of attitude with a desire to leave a self-governed pleasure-seeking life and submission to God's will as one is buried in the act of baptism, one cannot receive the Holy Spirit. Without baptism, being immersed and raised up, there is no rebirth.

A8 WHAT DO THE WORDS *WATER AND THE SPIRIT* IN JOHN 3:5 MEAN?

1. G. R. Beasley-Murray, *Baptism In The New Testament,* 228 n2.
2. Marcus Dods, *The Gospel Of St. John,* page 713.
3. W. E. Vine, Merrill F. Unger, William White, Jr., *Vine's Expository Dictionary of Biblical Words,* Thomas Nelson Publishers, Nashville Camden New York, 1985, pages 18 & 19.
4. M. R. Vincent, *Word Studies in the New Testament,* Mac Donald Publishing Company. P.O. Box 6006 Mac Dill AFB, Florida 33608, reprint of the 1888 printing, page 413.
5. C. F. Kiel, *Ezekiel Daniel,* Commentary on The Old Testament Volume 9, C.F. Kiel and F. Delitzsch, Translated by James Martin and M. G. Easton, Hendrickson Publishers, March 2006, page 148.

BIBLIOGRAPHY

1. Arndt, William F., and Gingrich, F. Wilbur, *A Greek-English Lexicon of the New Testament and Other Early Christian Literature,* The University of Chicago Press, Licensed to Zondervan Publishing House, Fourteenth Impression, 1973. Extra space before Licensed
2. Aylsworth, N.J., *Moral and Spiritual Aspects of Baptism*, Christian Publishing Company, St. Louis, 1902, Restoration Reprint Library, n.d.
3. Barclay, William, *The Letters of James and Peter revised edition, The Daily Study Bible Series,* The Westminster Press, Philadelphia, PA, 1976.
4. Barnes, Albert, *Barnes' Notes on the New Testament,* edited by Cobbin, Ingram, Complete and Unabridged in One Volume, Kregel Publications, Grand Rapids, Michigan, 1975.
5. Beale, Stephen, "7 Ways St. Jerome's Vulgate Helped Shape the Church, http://catholicexchange.com., September 30,2015.
6. Beasley-Murray, G.R., *Baptism In The New Testament*, William B. Eerdmans Publishing Company, Grand Rapids, Michigan, 1974
7. Boles, H. Leo, *New Testament Commentaries Luke*, Gospel Advocate Company, Nashville, Tenn., 1977.
8. Boles, H. Leo, *A Commentary on The Gospel According to Matthew*, Gospel Advocate Company, Nashville, Tenn., 1976.

9. Brents, T.W., *The Gospel Plan of Salvation*, Sixteenth Edition, Gospel Advocate Company, Nashville, TN, 1973 original printing 1874
10. Bruce, F.F., *The Epistle of Paul To The Romans An Introduction and Commentary*, Wm. B. Eerdmans Publishing Company, Grand Rapids, Michigan, 1969.
11. Bruce, F.F., The *Gospel of John*, Williams B. Eerdmans Publishing Company, Grand Rapids, Michigan, 1994.
12. Butler, Paul T., *The Gospel Of John, Vol. I,* Bible *Study Textbook* College Press, Joplin, Missouri, 1981.
13. Caton, N.T., *A Commentary and Exposition of the Epistles of James, Peter, John, and Jude,* Gospel Light Publishing Company, Delight, Arkansas, 1976,
14. Coffman, James Burton, *Commentary on 1 and 2 Corinthians*, Firm Foundation Publishing House, Box 610, Austin, Texas 78767, 1976.
15. Coffman, James Burton, *Commentary on John, Coffman Commentaries on the Old and New Testament,* https://www.studylight.org/commentaries/bcc/john-1.html., Abilene, Texas, USA, 1983-1999.
16. Cotham, Perry B., *Conversion,* published by Perry B. Cotham, 1976.
17. Delitzsch, F., *Volume 7 Isaiah, Commentary On The Old Testament* by C.F. Keil and F. Delitzsch,, Translated by James Martin, Hendrickson Publishers, March 2006.

18. Dods, Marcus, *The Gospel of St. John,* Volume One II, *The Expositor's Greek New* Testament edited by W. Robertson Nicoll, WM. B. Eerdmans Publishing Company, Grand Rapids, Michigan, reprinted 1974
19. Ferguson, Everett, *Church History Early and Medieval,* Second Edition, Biblical Press, 1966.
20. Ferguson, Everett, *Early Christians Speak Faith and Life in the First Three Centuries Revised Edition*, ACU Press, Abilene Christian University, Abilene, TX, 1987
21. Fields, Wilbur, *Philippians Colossians Philemon, Bible Study Textbook,* College Press, Joplin, Missouri, 1969.
22. Foster, R.C., *Studies in the Life of Christ*, Baker Book House, Grand Rapids, Michigan, 1975.
23. Fowler, Harold, *The Gospel of Matthew* Bible Study Textbook Series, Volume 1, College Press. Joplin. Missouri, 1981.
24. Fudge, Edward, *Our Man in Heaven An Exposition of the Epistle to the Hebrews*, Baker Book House, Grand Rapids, Michigan, 1974.
25. Halley, Henry H., *Halley's Bible Handbook,* Zondervan Publishing House, Grand Rapids, Michigan, 1965.
26. Harrub, Brad, *Convicted A Scientist Examines the Evidence for Christianity,* Focus Press, Inc.: 2011.
27. Hendriksen, William, *New Testament Commentary, Exposition of the Gospel According to Luke*, Baker Academic, Grand Rapids, Michigan, 1978.

28. Hendriksen, William, *New Testament Commentary, Exposition of the Gospel According to Matthew*, Baker Academic, Grand Rapids, Michigan, 1978.
29. Hendriksen, William, *New Testament Commentary, Exposition of Paul's Epistle to the Romans*, Baker Academic, Grand Rapids, Michigan, 2007.
30. Hendriksen, William, *New Testament Commentary, Galatians, Ephesians, Philippians, Colossians, and Philemon*, Baker Academic, Grand Rapids, Michigan, 1978.
31. Howard, V.E., *New Testament Conversions*, Central Printers and Publishers, 4107 White's Ferry Road, West Monroe, Louisiana, 1980.
32. Jackson, Wayne, *Revelation: Jesus Christ's Final Message of Hope, Selected Studies from The Apocalypse*, Christian Courier Publications, Inc., 7809 N. Pershing Avenue, Stockton, CA 95207, 2004.
33. Jividen, Jimmy, *Glossolalia from God or man?*, Star Bible Publications, 1971.
34. Johnson, B.W., *Vision of the Ages,* Gospel Light Publishing Company, Delight, Arkansas, n.a.
35. Johnson, Robert L., *The Letter of Paul to the Galatians,* The Living Word Commentary, R.B. Sweet Co., Inc., Austion, Texas, 1969.
36. Keil, C.F., *Volume 9 Ezekiel Daniel, Commentary On The Old Testament* by C.F. Keil and F. Delitzsch, by C.F. Keil, Translated by James Martin, Hendrickson Publishers, March 2006.

37. Lanier, Jr., Roy H., *Epistles of John, Notes on 1,2,3 John*. Quality Publications, P.O. Box 1060, Abilene, Texas, 79604-1060, 1992.
38. Lanier, Sr., Roy H., *The Timeless Trinity for the Ceaseless Centuries,* Denver, Colorado, 1974.
39. Lewis, Jack P., *The Gospel According to Matthew, Part I, 1:1-13:52*, The *Living Word Commentary* Sweet Publishing Company, Austin, Texas, 1975.
40. Lightfoot, J.B., *The Apostolic Fathers,* Edited and Completed by J.R. Harmer, Baker Book House, Grand Rapids, Michigan, 1974.
41. Marshall, Alfred, *The Interlinear Greek-English New Testament*, Regency Reference Library, Zondervan Publishing House, Grand Rapids, Michigan, 1958.
42. Mattox, F.W., *The Eternal Kingdom,* revised and with additional chapters by McRay, John, Gospel Light Publishing Company, Delight, Arkansas, 1961.
43. May, Jr., Cecil, *Bible Questions & Answers,* The Magnolia Messenger, Volume 42 – Number 2, Summer 2020.
44. Mayor, Joseph B., *The Epistle Of St. James the Greek Text with Introduction Notes and Comments,* Camb., Litt.D. Dubl., Second Edition, Baker Book House, Grand Rapids, Michigan, 1978 from the 1897 edition.
45. McCurley, Chris, *The Church Cherishes The Plan Of Salvation*, 2012 Bear Valley Lectures, *What's Right With The Church,* edited by Neal Pollard, A

Publication of the Bear Valley Bible Institute of Denver, printed by Sheridan Books, Inc., 2012.
46. McGarvey, J.W., and Pendleton, Philip Y., *Thessalonians, Corinthians, Galatians, and Romans, The Standard Bible Commentary,* The Standard Publishing Foundation, Cincinnati, Ohio.
47. McGuiggan, Jim, *The God Of The Towel,* Howard Publishing Co., West Monroe, Louisiana, 1997.
48. McGuiggan, Jim, *The Book of Revelation,* International Biblical Resources, Lubbock, Texas, 1967.
49. McGuiggan, Jim, *The Book of Romans, Looking Into The Bible Series,* Montex Publishing Company, Lubbock, Texas, 1982.
50. McKinley, Mike, *Passion,* The Good Book Company, 2013.
51. McMillan, Earle, *The Gospel According to Mark,* The Living Word Commentary, edited by Everett Ferguson, Sweet Publishing Company, Austin, Texas, 1973, page 191.
52. Miller, Dave, *Baptism & the Greek Made Simple,* Apologetics Press, Inc., 230 Landmark Drive, Montgomery, AL 36117, 2019.
53. Milligan, R., *New Testament Commentary Vol. IX. – Epistle To The Hebrews,* Gospel Advocate Co., Nashville, Tenn., 1974.
54. Milligan, R., *The Great Commission of Jesus Christ to His Twelve Apostles,* Lexington, KY, J.B. Morton & Company 1873, Restoration Reprint Library, n.d.

55. Mormonism Research Ministry, *Baptism for the Dead Definition,* http://www.mrm.org/MormonismResearchMinistry.
56. Murray, Andrew, *Abide in Christ,* Barbour and Company, Inc., Uhrichsville, Ohio, 1992.
57. Nichols, Gus, *Speaking The Truth In Love,* Nichols Bros. Publishing Co., Waxahachie, Texas, 1956.
58. Pack, Frank, *The Gospel According to John, Part I 1:1-10:42, The Living Word Commentary,* Sweet Publishing Company, Austin, Texas, 1975.
59. Pack, Frank, *The Living Word Commentary The Gospel According to John, Part II, 11:1-21:25, The Living Word Commentary,* Sweet Publishing Company, Austin, Texas, 1975.
60. Peake, A.S., *The Epistle to the Colossians,* Volume Three V, *The Expositor's Greek New Testament* edited by W. Robertson Nicoll, WM. B. Eerdmans Publishing Company, Grand Rapids, Michigan, reprinted 1974.
61. Oberst, Bruce, *Letters from Peter,* Bible Study Textbook Series, College Press, Joplin, Missouri, April 1979.
62. Owen, Dan R., *The Righteousness of God Study Notes on Romans,* Bear Valley School of Biblical Studies, Denver, Colorado, 1984.
63. Ramm, Bernard, *Protestant Biblical Interpretation,* Third Revised Edition, Baker Books, A Division of Baker Book House Co., Grand Rapids, Michigan 49516, 2005.

64. Randall, Frederic, *The Epistle to the Galatians,* The Expositor's Greek Testament, Volume III, Edited by W. Robertson Nicoll, Wm. B. Eerdmans Publishing Company, Grand Rapids, Michigan, 1974.
65. Rebaptdude, Puritan Board, http://www.puritanboard.com/threads/immersion-questions.34598/..July 19, 2008
66. Reese, Gareth L., *New Testament History Acts,* College Press, Joplin, Missouri, 1983.
67. Salmond, S.D.F., *The Epistle to the Ephesians,* The Expositor's Greek New Testament, Volume III, edited by W. Robertson Nicoll, Wm. B. Eerdmans Publishing Company, Grand Rapids, Michigan, 1974.
68. Sheffield, C.M., Puritan Board, http://www.puritanboard.com/threads/Luther:ImmersiontheBestMode of Baptism.97883/., April 15, 2019, Martin Luther, *The Babylonian Captivity of the Church.*
69. Smith, F LaGard, *Baptism The Believer's Wedding Ceremony*, Cotswold Publishing, 2013 by 21st Century Christian 2809 12th Ave S, Nashville, TN 37204
70. Smith, Nelson, *An Analysis of Sin*, Western Christian Foundation, P.O. Drawer W., Wichita Falls, Texas 76308.
71. Strobel, Lee, *The Case for a Creator,* Zondervan, Willow. 2004.
72. Strong, Augustus Hopkins, *Systematic Theology*, Three Volumes in One, Fleming H. Revell

Company, Old Tappan, New Jersey. Thirtieth Printing, 1976.
73. Tenney, Merrill C., *Galatians: The Charter of Christian Liberty*, Revised and Enlarged Edition, WM. B. Eerdmans Publishing Co, Grand Rapids, Michigan, 1975.
74. Thomas, Robert L., Th. D., General Editor, *New American Standard Exhaustive Concordance of The Bible,* The Lockman Foundation, Holman, Nashville, Tennessee, 1980, Greek Dictionary, page 1650.
75. *The Bible Visual Resource Book for Do-It-Yourself Bible Scholars,* Regal Books A Division of Gospel Light Publications, Ventura, California, U.S.A., 1989.
76. Vincent, M. R., *Word Studies in the New Testament,* Mac Donald Publishing Company. P.O. Box 6006 Mac Dill AFB, Florida 33608, reprint of the 1888 printing, page 413.
77. Vine, W.E., Unger, Merrill F., and White Jr., William, *Vine's Expository Dictionary of Biblical Words*, Thomas Nelson Publishers, Nashville, Camden, New York, 1985
78. Weed, Michael R., The *Letters of Paul to The Ephesians, the Colossians, and Philemon, The Living Word Commentary,* Editor Evertt Ferguson, R.B. Sweet Co., Inc., Austin, Texas, 1971.
79. Winder, Frances Joseph, *That They May Be Won*, and Morgan, Carey E., *The Harvest Is White*, and Thornton, B.W., 1923, Restoration Reprint Library.

80. Zodhiates, Spiros, *The Pursuit of Happiness*, AMG Press, Chattanooga, TN., 1981.

RECOMMENDED BOOKS FOR ADDITIONAL STUDY

Baptism & the Greek Made Simple by Dave Miller, Apologetics Press, Inc., 230 Landmark Drive, Montgomery, AL 36117, 2019.

Baptism In The New Testament by G. R. Beasley-Murray, William B. Eerdmans Publishing Company, Grand Rapids, Michigan, 1974.

Baptism The Believer's Wedding Ceremony by F. LaGard Smith, Cotswold Publishing, 21st Century Christian, 2809 12th Ave S., Nashville, TN 37204, 2013.

www.ingramcontent.com/pod-product-compliance
Lightning Source LLC
Chambersburg PA
CBHW061632040426
42446CB00010B/1380